Trouble

— ON —

Scioto's Waters

Trouble
— ON —
Scioto's Waters

Soldiers, Frontiersmen, & Native Americans, 1725–1815

JANET S. SHAILER

ORANGE *frazer* PRESS
Wilmington, Ohio

ISBN 978-1949248-364

Published for the copyright holder by:

Orange Frazer Press

37½ West Main St.

P.O. Box 214

Wilmington, OH 45177

For price and shipping information, call: 937.382.3196

Or visit: www.orangefrazer.com

Book and cover design by Kelly Schutte and Orange Frazer Press

Illustrations by Bonnie Young

Maps drawn by William Howison

Photos by Janet Shailer

Cover Image *Hawk's Nest* by Daniel Garber, 1917, Cincinnati Art Museum

The statue of Tecumseh depicted on the back cover is located outside of the Springfield Museum of Art. The sculptor is Michael Major of Urbana, Ohio.

Library of Congress Control Number: 2020921618

First Printing

To Colonel William Crawford and, to Tecumseh

Acknowledgments

This book would not be possible without two important institutions—the tremendous Ohio public library system and the inspiration of our state and local historical societies. They are both terrific resources for anyone wanting to study the Native Americans of Ohio and other topics.

I would like to thank the following libraries in particular: Southwest Public, Pickaway County Public, Bucyrus Public, and Columbus Metro Libraries. I would like to thank the archaeologists at the Ohio History Connection, and Linda Pansing in particular, for a chance to view the magnificent Stringtown Collection of Stemmed Lanceolates and for additional information on local mounds.

I would also like to thank the Columbus Metro Parks for all their efforts to preserve our natural resources, especially Battelle Darby Creek Metro Park and Nature Center and Scioto Grove Metro Park.

Central Ohio has a wealth of museums and organizations which are great sources of information, including the Welcome Center and Museum in Grove City, the Genealogy Society of Pickaway County in Circleville, and the Springfield Art Museum in Springfield.

Several people were most helpful in the writing of this book. They are: Reference Librarian Karen Lane, Assistant Director Bethanne Johnson, and Director Mark Shaw of Southwest Public Libraries, plus the following members of the Southwest Franklin County Historical Society—Steve Jackson, Linda Lewis, Barbara Howison, John Hines, Bev Babbert, Janet Garza, Keith Stenerson, Mike Esposito, Joan Eyerman, and Kelly Sutherland of the city of Grove City.

Individuals who provided either artifacts or assistance for this book include: John and Linda Worthington, Robert and Vicki Johnson, the Haughn family, Alan T. Seese, Robert C. Seese, Greg Kingsbury, Ken Milligan, Bill Graul, Sue Hamilton, Brent Eberhard, Michael Leach and Rick Palsgrove.

I would especially like to thank Prof. Christine B. Morris, American Indian Studies Coordinating Adviser at The Ohio State University's College of Arts and Sciences, for reviewing this book. In addition, I am grateful to Grove City High School and Bowling Green State University for nurturing my natural curiosity into my love for journalism and history.

A special thanks to artist Bonnie Young and to the late William Howison for his work on local Shawnee history.

As always, my family is my biggest inspiration and support system for which I am forever grateful—my husband John (Jack), my son John (Jay) and his wife Allison, my daughter Anna Kathryn, and my grandsons Alexander, Evan and Nathan Shailer.

To all those historic figures who have come before us in the rich history of Ohio, I say (as the Ottawa would say) "Wawanee, Wawanee" (Thank you, Thank you).

Table of Contents

Foreword

I was born in 1949 as the fourth generation in my family to live in a small Ohio farm town nestled between the Scioto River and Big Darby Creek. In high school, I used to hear boys in my class talk about the Indian arrowheads and artifacts they would find on their fathers' or grandfathers' farms. I found this captivating. It was not until 1974 when a family member found an Indian arrowhead next to my front door located one mile west of the Scioto River that the idea for this book germinated. It made me want to study Native Americans who believe they are the descendants of the earthwork builders and where their spirits are still alive. It is their homeland.

The Native Indians knew Ohio country was a special place and they helped to make it so. I believe in order to understand the history of a great people, we must thoroughly study them. Their history is a deep and captivating portrait of the human spirit.

Native Americans entered what is now central Ohio about 8,000–10,000 years ago and considered it their own. For people interested in both Prehistoric and Eastern Woodland Indians, the Middle Ohio Valley is an archaeologist's goldmine. The Ohio Historical and Archaeological Society estimated in the 1880s there were once 10,000 mounds and earthworks in Ohio alone. Urban development has left us with few remaining sites to see and explore.

In central Ohio, the Ohio History Connection has documented dozens of Prehistoric and Eastern Woodland sites all along the edges of the Scioto River. In my township alone (Jackson Township/Franklin County), archaeological maps show dozens of Native American sites along the edges of this waterway.

The area between Darby Creek and the Scioto River was once a cradle of Prehistoric and Woodland activity. This area has artifacts from the Paleo-Indians, Adena, Hopewell, and Fort Ancient Cultures. Later, Woodland Indians were also prevalent. The Scioto River watershed provided plenty of game for hunting and the fertile soil allowed Native American women to grow corn, beans, and squash—the "three sisters."

The Scioto River, which runs through the center of Franklin County, was a major highway for many Native Americans, including the Shawnee, Wyandot, Seneca, Delaware, Ottawa, and Miami. Other creeks in the Scioto River basin were also important for development. On the western side of Franklin County lies Big Darby Creek, another important transportation artery for several tribes. This waterway was used by the Shawnee on their way to camps in the Pickaway Plains. In the eastern part of Franklin County, Alum Creek runs south from Mt. Gilead and joins Big Walnut and Blacklick Creeks in (now) Three Creeks Metro Park. The Adena built at least seven mounds in the Alum Creek Valley.

From 1754–1814 fighting raged within the state between Ohio Indians and their adversaries. By 1843, the last of the Native Americans left the state after the signing of the Treaty with the Wyandots. A mere 18 years later the Civil War would start.

Some sagas about the first Ohioans have not been kind to them. As a 50-year professional journalist, I wanted to be as fair as possible to both sides of the story. As an amateur historian, I wanted to provide a slice of Ohio history for those who want to pursue it further. I use the term "Indian" in many circumstances due to the volume of research material that names them so. Though I have spent countless hours researching this book, I apologize for any errors.

Parts of this book are meant as a guide for people to start their own research on the "First Ohioans." As a person of endless curiosity, I wanted to provide an inspirational guide for those who want to visit sites where Native Americans once thrived to go and do so. Additionally, the Ohio History Connection and the State Library of Ohio have created a digital collection of historical material called the Ohio Memory project. To access it, go to Ohiomemory.org.

Trouble on Scioto's Waters

Trouble

— ON —

Scioto's Waters

1
Fire and Ice

The history of Native Americans in Ohio country can be condensed to three simple words—fire and ice.

Paleo-Indians first walked across North America during the Pleistocene Ice Age at least 30,000 years ago just as melting glaciers formed natural transportation routes such as rivers and lakes. These waters became transit crossings that first brought nomadic hunter-gatherers to Ohio country. Clovis people roamed the valleys, ravines, and swamps using hand-carved spear points to kill elephant-sized mastodons and wooly mammoths who slogged to grazing spots everywhere from Lake Erie to the Ohio River. These lumbering mammals became extinct about 10,000 years ago, as did long-horn bison and giant ground sloths, but the early humans remained and adapted.

By 800 B.C., the pre-historic Indians, termed the "Adena Culture" by Anglo scholars, prospered and became entwined in the evolution of Ohio. They were followed by people who researchers titled "Hopewell" and "Fort Ancient People." Though they did not have a written language, they left monuments to their existence in the form of petroglyphs, mounds, and major geometric earthworks. Ohio contains a greater number of prehistoric remains than any other equal area in the Mississippi Valley. The valley between the two Miami rivers as well as the Scioto and Muskingum valleys were natural settings for prehistoric man. It is in this region that we find the principal monuments of these early people.

For some unknown reason, they left Ohio country by the 17th century. By the 1660s, Ohio was an untamed and uninhabited tangle of wilderness, complete with prairie grass, murky bogs, and thick forests. Only a handful of British and French fur trappers and traders braved this lonely frontier. It would take until the 1720s for other humans—Eastern Woodland Indians looking to hunt—to trickle along the Great Lakes until reaching the Cuyahoga River Valley. Here they found rich soil, endless hunting grounds, room to roam, and an inhabitable climate. Natural resources such as flint used for making spear points and limestone used for creating tools were abundant. It was the perfect setting and the new beginning of Ohio country. By the mid-18th century the Ohio Valley had become a patchwork of tribal homelands.

All Ohio tribes shared the Eastern Woodland Indian culture. They are so named because they and the earthwork builders lived near lakes and streams, and Ohio country was exceedingly favorable to forest life. Every aspect of their lives—food, shelter, weapons, tools, and clothing—came from the forest. These first Ohioans were hunters who found an abundance of deer, bear, beaver, otter, elk, and wild turkey. The women and children found plenty of nuts, berries, and a fruit called black haw. They made their clothes from the skins of their kill, created villages, and had a social structure and spiritual order.

And that is where the fire comes in. The Ohio country Native Americans wanted only to hunt, fish, protect their families, and live their lifestyle. It would not take long for clashes to begin with the French, English, and eventually the new Americans. There would be violence, torture, and needless death on both sides. In one of the most heinous crimes on earth, some people were burned at the stake.

We will study three major tribes who inhabited Ohio country for over a hundred years beginning in the 1720s and, to a lesser extent, four others. All of them either lived in central Ohio or had at least a passing interaction with those who lived along the Scioto River watershed. They are:

Tribe	Language
Miami (Myaamia)	Algonquin
Shawnee (Shawanese)	Algonquin
Huron-Wyandot (Wyandotte)	Iroquoian

And to a lesser extent:

Tribe	*Language*
Delaware (Lenape)	Algonquin
Huron (Erie)	Iroquoian
Ottawa (branch of Ojibwe)	Algonquin
Seneca-Cayuga (also known as Mingo)	Iroquoian

Most of the Native American tribes did not have a written language.

Miami: This powerful tribe occupied all of northern Indiana and entered Ohio country around the 1720s from the Wabash and Maumee rivers as one of the first tribes in Ohio. Soon they claimed the territory east of the Great/Little Miami rivers all the way to the Scioto River. The hospitable terrain allowed them to build villages and open trade with the British at Pickawillany—a trading post at present day Piqua near the portage to the St. Marys River. The word "Piqua" means "man who arose from ashes." Their principal villages were along the head waters of two Miami (Great and Little) rivers and the Miami of the Lake (Maumee). "Myaamia" means "downstream people."

Shawnee (Shawanese): This tribe established villages around the 1730s along the Ohio River and Scioto Valley. The Shawnee re-established this connection after disappearing from Ohio country and settling in Kentucky, Georgia, and Alabama. The name "Shawunogi" means 'southerner.' Their villages were mostly along the lower Scioto River in (now) Pickaway and Ross Counties. The center of Shawnee culture, however, was at the mouth of the Scioto River at Lower Shawnee Town (Portsmouth). Another principal village was Upper Shawnee Town (Chillicothe/Hopeton). By 1752 it was a tribal center. The Shawnee looked upon the Delaware as "their grandfathers." They had at least four villages near or between the Scioto River and Big Darby Creek (Cornstalk's Town, Nonhelema's Town, Kispoko, and Pucksinwah's Town) and one west of Darby Creek on Deer Creek called Blue Jacket's Town (now Williamsport). Later, Blue Jacket moved to another village which became Bellefontaine. In the western part of the state, the Shawnee village of Piqua had about 4,000 people. The Kickapoo tribe's spoken language closely resembled that of the Shawnee.

Wyandot or Wyandotte: Historians generally agree that Wyandots were the fiercest and most powerful tribe inhabiting Ohio, if not the Midwest. This branch of the Hurons originated in the Georgian Bay in Canada, which was once known as "New France." They were related to the Iroquois Confederacy but were driven away and settled across northern Ohio. Their principal village, however, was in (now) Upper Sandusky with other villages in (now) Crawford, Marion, and Wyandot Counties. They also had villages as far south as Ross County. The Wyandot social structure was divided into four groups: family, gens, phratry, and tribe. One of their large villages, known as Tarhe Town or Crane Town, was in (now) Lancaster.

Delaware (Lenape): This tribe was originally from the Delaware River Valley but migrated west due to European settlement along the East Coast. They moved mostly along the Tuscarawas and Muskingum River Valleys in the 1770s. Many were converted to Christianity by Moravian missionaries. Their language was closely related to the Miami. One of their villages was Maguck Town (near Circleville), which at one time was occupied by Shawnee.

Huron: These tribal members were close to the Wyandots originally from Quebec. Their Wyandot language is related to the Iroquois language and they may at one time been part of the Iroquois Confederacy. They were known for their Mohawk hair style which the French thought made them look like the mane of a wild boar.

Ottawa: This tribe once occupied a region along the Ottawa River in Canada and was pushed west by the Iroquois, eventually resettling near Detroit after 1701. They drifted into the northwest Ohio country in the 1720s and built villages on the lower Maumee River and along Maumee Bay. Ottawa is the Algonquin word for "trader."

Seneca (Mingo): This tribe is related to the Seneca of New York but lived along the Sandusky River in Ohio. They were one of the most powerful members of the Iroquois confederacy and were made up of members from several tribes. They were known as Onondowagan—"Keepers of the Western Door." They were of the great Haudenosawnee Confederation. The Erie Indians were absorbed into this band of the Iroquois Nation. Mingo is a general term referring to members of the Iroquois Confederacy (Six Nations), primarily Seneca and Cayuga, who had moved from their lands in upstate New York into the Cuyahoga River Valley. They are also known as the Ohio Seneca or Ohio Iroquois. After the end of the Beaver Wars around 1701, the Seneca settled in the eastern part of Ohio country, mostly around today's Steubenville area. During the

🔺 *The Scioto River. The Scioto River is 231 miles long and runs from Portsmouth in Scioto County to Auglaize County in northwest Ohio. It was a major transportation artery for Native Americans, frontiersmen, and soldiers.*

American Revolutionary War, many Seneca made their homes with the Wyandots. There were many Seneca-Mingo villages along the Scioto and Sandusky rivers with one of the largest villages, Pluggy's Town, located in (now) Delaware, Ohio. Some historians have said the term "Mingo" was used as a derogatory word.

Into the land that Native Americans considered the perfect hunting ground tumbled turmoil between the British and French who laid claim to it and tribes who were determined to deter them. The first European credited with entering Ohio country was Frenchman Rene-Robert Cavelier, Sieur de LaSalle, who sailed the Great Lakes region after the Mohawks told him of a great river named the Ohio that flowed into the Mississippi. The French saw tremendous advantage in using the Ohio River as a critical link between Canada (New France) and the Mississippi Valley.

So prized did the Ohio country appear to the French that Capt. Pierre-Joseph de Celeron de Bienville left Montreal with a large party of Canadians and Indians to claim Ohio country in 1740 by burying metal plaques in the ground at the junction of the six tributaries along the Ohio River.

Fire and Ice

The French were followed by the British who traveled trade routes into the land of the Iroquois and then crossed the Allegheny Mountains. Not long afterwards, the British staked their claim to the Ohio country. A British settler named Christopher Gist surveyed along the Muskingum and Ohio rivers for the Ohio Company, which consisted of Virginia land speculators. In 1753, Gist and a young Virginian named George Washington surveyed the area using a canoe as their mode of travel. The colony of Virginia bordered the Ohio River to the south. Kentucky would not become a state until 1792 and West Virginia would not become a state until 1863.

Both the French and British courted favor with the Native Americans in Ohio country as trading partners. For the most part, Indians did not take sides but angled for who would best benefit them. Once the French were defeated, Ohio Indians realized the French trading posts would become British ones. The British sought superiority in the region through trade while not promoting settlements. The Native Americans wanted trade as well as the freedom to roam and hunt and they would not accept anything less. Some tribes thought the land was their birthright. Some British felt the Ohio Indians should be subservient. It was inevitable that blood was going to be sacrificed.

Between 1740–1840, came the French and Indian War (1754–1763), the Revolutionary War (1776–1783), and the War of 1812 (1812–1815). As the last of the Native Americans were leaving Ohio in 1843, the brutal American Civil War was only eighteen years away.

When the Continental Army under George Washington defeated the British in the Revolutionary War, Ohio country Indian tribes had to contend with the brazen Americans who were determined to move into the rich beauty of what is now the Buckeye state.

Ohio country became a caldron in the clash between the American settlers and the Native Americans. It is a story filled with jealousy and revenge, missionaries and spies, traders and traitors. Along the way there are shifting loyalties, broken promises, mysteries, and, most of all, a sense of entitlement. There were proud warriors, ambitious frontiersmen, and determined soldiers.

Most of them had one thing in common—they used the Scioto River watershed in the heart of Ohio country and the Ohio River at its edge as a major means of travel. Eventually, in 1803, Ohio would become the first state to be created out of territory belonging to the Union.

It is a story conceived in struggle. It is the story of the birth of Ohio.

Additional Information

The French government donated a monument of Celeron de Bienville to the city of Marietta, Ohio at the spot of the discovery of one of his metal plates along the Ohio River.

The only surviving lead plate from Celeron's exploration and declaration of conquest along the Ohio River is displayed at the Virginia Museum of History & Culture in Richmond, Virginia.

2

Prehistoric Native Americans in the Scioto Basin

The following framework for the study of Native Americans will be useful for our study of the period known as prehistory, that is, before written records. It goes:

Paleo-Indian: 12000–7000 B.C.
Archaic Period: 8000–500 B.C.
Woodland Period: 1000 B.C.–A.D. 1000.
Late Prehistoric Period: A.D. 900–1650.

Evidence of Native Americans in every time frame from Paleo-Indian to the Late Prehistoric Period in the Ohio River Valley is, to quote a phrase, "mammoth." The Ohio State Archaeological and Historical Society in 1900 estimated there were once 10,000 mounds in the Middle Ohio Valley, including earthworks, mounds, and graves. Since then, modern archaeologists believe there may have been even more. It is estimated that about 1,000 of those mounds survive today with most erected about 2,000–3,000 years ago during the Woodland Period.

Archaeologist William Mills wrote in the late 19th century, "Ohio is the richest state, archaeologically speaking, in the Union." The remains of these ancient people in the Middle Ohio Valley have been found mostly along or near the Ohio River (between Pittsburgh and Louisville), the Scioto River, and both the Great and Little Miami rivers.

To have lived during these ancient times would have meant you were an infant in the ancient cradle of a great prehistoric people.

Paleo-Indians

Paleo-Indians, or Clovis culture people, lived during the final glacial period in the late Paleo or early Archaic period. Research shows that the first Americans came from Asia possibly as early as 20,000 years ago when the sea levels dropped during the glacial periods. A large land bridge, called Beringia, formed in southern Siberia and crossed to the Americas allowing the Paleo-Indians to travel to North America. In 2020, researchers from the Universidad Autonoma de Zacatecas, Mexico and the University of Oxford found evidence of human occupation in caves going even further back in time in the central-northern Mexican Highlands. Eventually people entered what is now the state of Ohio and Franklin County. They most likely lived in small groups called bands, each with their own territory. These bands did not build permanent settlements but often returned to the same camp sites during certain seasons.

Late Paleo people are known as the lanceolate makers. These hunting weapons were generally long and slender with a base an inch or so wide. One theory of why the lanceolates were developed is that the animals available in area forests (such as elk and deer) could be killed with points that did not require deep penetration. The Early Paleo or Late Archaic people liked to camp on low ridges above water sources such as lakes and rivers. They also needed flint or chert to make their weapons and Ohio country had plenty of natural resources. Two major sources of flint, for example, were Flint Ridge (Vanport) and Coshocton (Upper Mercer). They made several varieties of fluted points.

Into central Ohio the Native Americans would soon nestle in a cradle between the Scioto River to the east and the Big Darby Creek to the west where the climate was mild, water clean, natural resources bountiful, and game abundant.

Evidence of the Paleo-Indians' existence in Franklin County was discovered in the Jackson Township/Grove City area in 1952 by residents Ernest and Dorothy Good. The Goods found the largest collection of Plano points ever collected in Ohio while walking fields near the intersection of Stringtown Road and State Rt. 104. The Goods found dozens of lanceolate points that may be 6,000 years old. In this grouping were whole and fragmentary lanceolates and stemmed lanceolate points—some with a basal spur. This is known as the Stringtown Collection and continues to be studied by the Ohio History Connection in Columbus. The points were made from Mercer black flint and local Delaware chert from Columbus limestone. So unusual is this find that a point type has been named for the collection—the Stringtown Stemmed Lanceolates.

According to an article written by Robert Converse and Ernest Good in 1974 for "Ohio Archaeologist," several other cultures were also represented at this location. A tubular Adena pipe made of sandstone with rare engravings around the stem was found. Five pieces of gorgets that appear to be an Adena keyhole pendant were found there along with four plummets—two of them hematite. In addition, a portion of a Hopewell platform pipe was also found.

There is no doubt that the Stringtown site was particularly important to the prehistoric Indians and was used as an encampment near the Scioto River.

Adena

After the Paleo-Indians came the Woodland cultures to the Middle Ohio Valley. These people included the Adena Culture (800 B.C. to A.D. 100), the Ohio Hopewell Culture (100 B.C. to A.D. 500), and the Fort Ancient Culture (1000–1650 A.D.) Unfortunately, most of these mounds and villages have been destroyed due to modern development.

The Adena Culture developed in the Early Woodland Period. The name comes from Governor Thomas Worthington (Ohio's 6th governor serving 1814–1818) who built a home northwest of Chillicothe and called it "Adena." It is not the name of an Indian tribe. On the Worthington grounds was located a twenty-six-foot tall ancient burial mound. This Adena Mound site has all the features of an entire ancient culture (a type site) and the name was affixed to it. The Adena had an organized social order. They buried their dead in distinctive mounds that archaeologists have determined served as territorial markers. The Adena and Hopewell were the leading builders of geometric earthworks.

The Adena were hunter-gatherers who lived in small villages near gardens and began domesticating crops. They moved frequently to hunt the ever-moving animal herds. They were the first people to produce clay pottery in Ohio country. These vessels were made with thick walls used for cooking. The Adena also had an extensive trading network in order to seek raw materials such as mica and copper. From these materials they would create funerary objects such as bracelets, ear spools, gorgets, and weapons.

The Adena Culture eventually developed into the Hopewell Culture. The Hopewell (100 B.C. to A.D. 500) are not a specific Indian tribe but an archaeological term. The Hopewell way of life developed across the Midwest with Ohio country as the center around 2,000 years ago. They were master builders. Their mounds were bigger than Adena and their burials had more ceremony. The Fort Hill Earthworks located in Brush Creek Township in Highland County is one of the best-preserved ancient hilltop enclosures built by the Ohio Hopewell Culture.

The Woodland Period is known as the Age of the Moundbuilders. No mound building group built more mounds than the Adena and Ohio Hopewell. Mounds were built as enclosures of religious ceremonial life and monuments to the dead. The ancient Indians felt the world was full of spirits and evil forces that surrounded them in places like forests, rock piles, and waterways. The burial mounds were an expression of their faith. They placed cherished gifts to the dead such as tools, pottery, and ornaments in their mounds. There is evidence that at some point they turned from worshipping only animal deities to those who flew in the sky. Hawks, eagles, and owls had a special place in their hearts. They also were very precise in aligning earthworks with the sun during events such as the summer and winter solstice.

Hopewell

The Hopewell sought to create earthworks in the shape of circles, squares, and octagonals from approximately A.D. 1 and 400. The city of Circleville was built in 1810 over a large circular Hopewell earthwork 1,100 feet in diameter connected to a 900-foot square. This county seat was plotted perfectly in a circle by Daniel Dreisbach who placed the courthouse in the center. Later the town was reconstructed into a typical grid. Unfortunately, the mounds were destroyed with the new construction. The circular earthworks built by Hopewells are believed to have been used for ceremonial purposes. The original circle built in Circleville was located just to the east of the confluence of the Scioto River and Big Darby Creek.

The Great Hopewell Road from Newark to Chillicothe is being continuously studied by archaeologists. The road was a set of parallel earthen embankments about three feet high and 200 feet apart that extended from an opening in the octagonal earthworks at the Newark Earthworks down at least ten miles to the southwest. A portion of the road can be spotted from the air using sophisticated infrared photography. It is believed to have been a spiritual path sixty miles long. The Newark Earthworks were four square miles in length and show eight lunar alignments. The Hopewell measured the entire lunar cycle of 18.6 years.

The Hopewell had use of Vanport flint. They created artwork such as ornaments and earspools and also created large ceremonial blades. They utilized artistic expression in mounds, building some three stories tall.

The second largest conical mound east of the Mississippi River is the Miamisburg Mound in Miamisburg (Montgomery County). The Hopewell built this mound on a ridge above the Great Miami River and it is listed on the National Register of Historic Places. From the Hopewell, researchers have found copper axes and other kinds of copper jewelry.

The Hopewell also believed that animals and birds were spiritual guardians. In southern Ohio, small pipes carved by Hopewell craftsmen have been found that are in the shape of falcons and other animals.

The Hopewell made improvements in cultivating edible plants such as maygrass, knotweed, and goosefoot that provided nutrition to the Indians in addition to the nuts, fish, wild turkey, and deer of their diet. The development of earthenware pottery aided in their cooking.

Fort Ancient

The Fort Ancient Culture is considered Late Woodland Period. These people typically lived on bluffs or terraces near river valleys. Fort Ancient in Oregonia, Ohio is considered the most extensive prehistoric fortification in North America. Located in central Warren County, it sits on a 126-acre high plateau overlooking the Little Miami River. It is divided into three sections: Old Fort, Middle Fort, and New Fort. There are ravines on the east, west, and south sides of the earthworks which leads historians to believe it was a defensive structure. The walls were possibly twenty-feet high at one time, made mostly of earth and stone. It is believed that Native Americans from thirty–forty miles away came there to rendezvous for defensive or religious purposes.

Less than one-half mile from Fort Ancient are the remains of several small Indian villages (or hamlets) running along the river that would have served the Native Americans while they were hunting. There is evidence that bison once thrived on the western edge of the site.

Their villages were generally in a circular pattern surrounding a public place. Dwellings were probably wooden structures covered in plant matter or hide. They buried their dead outside the villages in mounds or limestone coffins.

At this time, the Native Americans began using vast acres of land to cultivate crops. Women worked the gardens by using marine shells as hoes to till the ground. They cultivated the "Three Sisters"—corn, beans, and squash—plus pumpkins. They created ceramic vessels with necks and handles.

Fort Ancient is a National Historic Landmark and Ohio's first state park. Archaeologists continue to do radio-carbon dating to determine if the Fort Ancient Culture built the magnificent Serpent Mound in Adams County. It could date back to 1070 A.D. There are seventy-one openings in the walls of Fort Ancient which are called "gateways."

The Late Woodland Culture all collected nuts and berries and hunted large and small animals. The edible plants and animals were readily available in overgrown clearings. Fishing in rivers and streams was especially important for this culture because they had many people to support over long periods of time. There is some evidence that the Shawnee were descended from the Fort Ancient people. We also do not know why the last of the Fort Ancient Culture left the Ohio country possibly as late as the early 17th century.

As new hand tools such as hoes, rakes, and shovels were developed, villages became much more stable because the women needed to constantly tend to their crops in the same area. From these people grinding stones and sandstone pestles were found. Elbow smoking pipes have also been discovered. Men wore breechclouts and sometimes slate gorgets. Women wore skirts. Members of the tribe used flint knives for hunting.

No one is certain what happened to the Fort Ancient Culture. There seems to be no evidence that they migrated out of Ohio country. Archaeologists are studying evidence that changes may have occurred due to a decline in soil fertility, not warfare or disease. Still, no one really knows.

Mounds

The trails connecting Lake Erie to the Ohio River passed through central Ohio and what is now Franklin County. Numerous Indian villages were located near the confluence of the Scioto and Olentangy rivers. Several mounds and numerous burial sites have been unearthed as Columbus and its suburbs were built. Archaeologists have documented dozens of sites in southern Franklin County alone skirting along the Scioto River. These include the mounds discovered in the late 1880s and documented by the Ohio Historical & Archaeology Society in the Ohio Archaeological & Historical Quarterly of 1888:

Location	Mound	About the Mound
Franklin Township	Anderson Mound	N/A
Hamilton Township	Hartman Farms Mound	N/A
	Thomas Clark Mound	50 feet in diameter
	W.N. Fisher farm	One mound
	C. Lahman farm	One mound
	A. O'Harra farm	Two mounds
	Robert Simpson farm	One mound
	W.T. Spangler farm	One mound
	E.J. Young farm	One mound

Ohio has several sites built by prehistoric Native Americans. The Newark area is a typical example of one of the great ceremonial centers. Items that have been found in the Hopewell sites suggest they had a vast trading network. For example, copper from the Great Lakes and mica from the southern Appalachian Mountains were found in burial sites. Other items found include tobacco pipes, Grizzly bear teeth, freshwater pearls, chert arrowheads, animal figurines, and jewelry. There is also evidence that the Ohio Hopewell may have built a pilgrimage route from the (now) Newark area to Chillicothe known as the Hopewell Road. It is possible they used this straight-line path to get flint at Flint Ridge in (now) Licking County. Flint Ridge has been called the "Great Indian Quarry of Ohio." All of Ohio's prehistoric Indians used this flint to make spears, small knives (bladelets), and arrow points. The Vanport flint found there is the official gemstone for the state of Ohio.

▲ *Serpent Mound. Serpent Mound in Adams County is the world's largest effigy mound and is one of the most celebrated sites in the Eastern Woodland Culture. The Shawnee called it the "Great Snake" and the Miami the "underwater panther." It is believed to be 900 years old.*

Another great mound builder center is Ross County. Mounds and earthworks were built in geometric forms such as circles, squares, octagons, and other shapes even though they did not have mathematical instruments.

Many of the following sites are written about in Mark J. Lynott's book *Hopewell Ceremonial Landscapes of Ohio* published in 2014 by Oxbow Books. Others have been written about by D.R. Gehlbach in *The Archaeology of Franklin County, Ohio* published in 1997. Some of these prehistoric Indian sites are listed below by the Ohio counties in which they were found:

Adams County

Serpent Mound: 3850 St. Rte. 73, Peebles, Ohio, 45660. This magnificent mound is one of the most celebrated sites in Eastern Woodland Culture. Built by the ancient American Indians, the world's largest effigy mound is an internationally known National Historic Landmark. The mound is in the shape of a long serpent. Three ancient burial mounds are nearby. Radiocarbon dating determined that the mound is approximately 900 years old. It is on a list for possible inclusion as one of UNESCO's World Heritage sites.

Delaware County

Highbanks Metro Park Mounds I and II: 9466 Columbus Pike, U.S. Route 23, Lewis Center, Ohio, 43035. There are two mounds believed to be Adena. They are also referred to as the Muma Mound and the Orchard Mound or the Selvey Mound. The mounds are in Highbanks Metro Park on the east bank of the Olentangy River in the southernmost part of Delaware County. They are listed on the U.S. Register of Historic Places.

Fairfield County

Cross Mound Park (also known as Tarlton Cross Mound): 11615 16th Road Southwest, Stoutsville, Ohio, 43154. This ancient earthwork in the shape of a plus sign or cross sits just west of Salt Creek, a tributary of the Scioto River. It may have been part of a sixty-two-mile pathway that once connected the Great Octagon Earthworks in New-

Shrum Mound a.k.a. Campbell Mound. *The Shrum Mound in Campbell Park on McKinley Ave. near Trabue Rd. on Columbus's westside was built by Adena between 800 B.C. to A.D. 100. This conical mound is 20-feet high and sits just west of the Scioto River.*

Voss Mound–Battelle–Darby Creek Park. The Voss Mound in Battelle-Darby Creek Metro Park can be accessed on the Ancient Trail near the confluence of the Big & Little Darby Creeks. Archaeologists believe it is the site of a village built by the Ft. Ancient Culture.

ark to Hopeton Earthworks in Chillicothe, which are in Hopewell Cultural National Historic Park. It is on the National Register of Historic Places.

Franklin County

Battelle-Darby Creek Metro Park: in Galloway. This 7,000-acre park stretches thirteen miles along the Big and Little Darby Creeks. These creeks have been designated as State and National Scenic rivers. The park includes forests, prairies, and wetlands. Among the trails are two that are connected to prehistoric Indians. They are: *The Ancient Trail,* a 1.9-mile trail that includes the Voss Mound. This mound is believed to be Fort Ancient Culture and covers a circular structure that experts think burned around A.D. 966. Archaeologists have used magnetometers to determine the layout of a village here without digging it up. They also found a path that the Native Americans used. It is located near the Ridge Picnic Area along the western arm of the Ancient Trail loop. The Tom Cannon Mound Trail has an Adena Mound a few feet north of the junction of Big and Little Darby Creeks. Finally, the Big Darby Nature Center, located at 1415 Darby Creek Drive, intersects two bison pastures. This is an excellent educational experience for children and adults. Native American artifacts are on display in the Nature Center.

Indian Mound Park: Obetz Road at Parsons Ave., Columbus, Ohio. Two loaf-shaped mounds that may be Hopewell. Also known as Shoaf Mounds.

Jeffers Mound: 6541 Plesenton Dr., Worthington, Ohio, 43085. It is believed to be either an Adena or Hopewell site with a ceremonial mound and earthworks built between 100 B.C.–A.D. 400. It was part of a larger area of earthworks on a bluff overlooking the Olentangy River. It is listed on the National Register of Historic Places.

Merion, Zencor, Scioto Trails: Columbus, Ohio. These are primarily late Woodland, possibly Fort Ancient culture, near the old Scioto Trails School site at 2951 S. High St. Dates are undetermined but most likely A.D. 1000 to 1200.

Shrum Mound (also known as the Campbell Mound): 3141 McKinley Ave., Columbus, Ohio, 43204. This mound is twenty-feet high and 100 feet in diameter and was built by the Adena Culture. It is in James E. Campbell Park on Columbus's Westside north of Trabue Road.

Other Franklin County sites reported as early as 1888 but have since been eliminated by urban growth are:

Ambos Mound: once located near the corner of Greenlawn and Thurman Avenues at S. High St. Believed to be Adena.

H.C. Cook farm: Clintonville, Ohio. Conical mounds sat at the junction of two creeks near Wynding Dr. that emptied into the Olentangy River. Excavated in 1953. Others near there were located on Rathbone Road, Webster Park, and Olentangy Village.

Joseph Ferris farm: Perry Township, Ohio. It's one mile north of the Dublin Bridge. It hosts three forts, one of which is eighty feet in diameter, with an entrance on the east side. Also found were two small mounds.

Mound Street Mound: Once located on the eastern side of the Scioto River at the southeast corner of High and Mound Streets in downtown Columbus, Ohio. It was believed to be forty feet high and 300 feet in diameter.

Toepfner Mound (also called the Anderson Mound): Once located at the corner of Riverside Drive and Grandview Ave. in Columbus, Ohio. It was built by the Adena Culture but was leveled in 1954.

Greene County

Indian Mound Reserve: 2750 U.S. Route 42E, Cedarville, Ohio, 45314. There are 169 acres of geological structures and over eight miles of hiking trails, including the Mound Trail leading to the Williamson Mound. The park has the largest network of paved trails in the U.S.

Highland County

Fort Hill Earthworks & Nature Preserve: 13614 Ft. Hill Road, Hillsboro, Ohio, 45133. Built by Ohio Hopewell, Fort Hill has a well-preserved enclosure that is like the one at Fort Ancient. The hilltop earthworks are only accessible by hiking to the top. Also, the Circle Earthwork is in a field on the south side of the park. The park has 1,300 acres with a mature forest and great hiking trails.

Licking County

The Alligator Mound: on Bryn du Drive off Newark-Granville Road (County Road 539), near Granville, Ohio, was built in A.D. 800–1200 by the Fort Ancient Culture. It overlooks Raccoon Creek Valley and resembles an opossum or a panther more than an alligator. It is likely a ceremonial site as it was not used for burial.

Flint Ridge State Memorial: St. Rte. 668 near Glenford, Ohio. It is easily accessible running nine miles long and three miles wide and known as one of the best quarries in North America. Flint was extracted from the Paleo-Indian Period up to Historic times. It was an important source of flint for the Hopewell and is known as the "Great Indian Quarry of Ohio." There is a museum at 15300 Flint Road, Glenford, Ohio, 43739.

Huffman Mound (Tippett Mound): Heath/Newark, Ohio. This twenty-foot-high mound is located on the Taft Reserve on Flint Ridge Road on the southeast side of Newark, between Newark and I-70 on Route 312. A tubular tobacco pipe was found near the center of the mound. It is believed to be Adena.

The Newark Earthworks: Newark and Heath, Ohio. They include the Great Circle Earthworks, the Octagon Earthworks, and the Wright Earthworks. They were built by the Hopewell and are National Historic Landmarks. The Newark Earthworks system is the largest geometric earthwork complex in the world. The Great Circle can be accessed from Hebron Road. and is an open park with a small museum. The Octagon is on the grounds of the Moundbuilders Country Club, 125 N. 33rd St., but access is restricted to a parking lot and viewing platform. In 2006, the State of Ohio designated the earthwork complex as "the official prehistoric monument of the state."*

Ross County

Adena Mound: Chillicothe, Ohio. This is buried beneath a housing development at Lake Ellensmere on the northwest edge of Chillicothe. The Adena Mound gave its name to the Adena Culture and was originally twenty-six feet high with a circumference of 445 feet.

Hopewell Culture National Historic Park: 16062 St. Rte. 104, Chillicothe, Ohio, 45601. Six major earthworks cover nearly 1,200 acres near the confluence of Paint Creek and the Scioto River. These are: Mound City Group, Hopeton Earthworks, Hopewell Mound Group, Seip Earthworks, High Banks Earthworks, and Spruce Hill. This is the largest collection of Hopewell culture burial mounds in eastern North America. There is a Visitor's Center at Mound City, 16062 State Route 104, featuring the Hopewell culture.*

Story Mound State Memorial: Chillicothe, Ohio, 45601. This Adena mound is on the east side of Delano Ave. within a small park area. The Story Mound was originally about the same size as the Adena Mound which is one mile to the northwest. It is twenty feet high and ninety-five feet in diameter and is the first documented example of a circular Adena timber building discovered in 1897.

Warren County

Fort Ancient State Park: 6123 OH-350, Oregonia, Ohio, 45054. The park features 18,000 feet of man-made earthen embankment and is the largest prehistoric hilltop enclosure in North America. Fort Ancient was built by the Hopewell on a wooded bluff 235 feet above the Little Miami River. There is also an Adena site on the grounds.*

*The Hopewell Culture National Park, Mound City Group, Seip Earthworks, High Banks Earthworks, Hopeton Earthworks, Newark Earthworks State Memorial, and Fort

Ancient State Memorial are collectively referred to as "Hopewell Ceremonial Earthworks." They are the United States' first Ohio-centric bid for UNESCO (United Nations Educational, Scientific, and Cultural Organization) World Heritage Site status. Serpent Mound is in another location also being considered for a UNESCO World Heritage Site.

Other Related Sites–Prehistoric Petroglyphs of Ohio

The word Petroglyph is Greek for "rock art." Archaeologists have found that mounds were constructed of earth or stone (sometimes mixed). Items that have been found in mounds include pottery, bone and copper beads, and mica.

These petroglyphs were created by picking, pecking, carving, or abrading the rock surface in the form of art. Experts estimate that Ohio's petroglyphs were carved between A.D. 900–1750. Petroglyphs have been found as far north as Kelleys Island and as far south as Lawrence County near the Ohio River.

James L. Swauger, in his book *Petroglyphs of Ohio* (dated 1984), stated that he studied petroglyphs in the Buckeye state for 16 years. Almost all the sixty-one reported petroglyphs in his book were found in the eastern part of Ohio with the largest number found in Adams County. Images include those of animals, fish, reptiles, humans, and

Limestone circle—Fort Ancient. The Fort Ancient people created limestone circles for certain ceremonial events. This one is in Ft. Ancient State Park, which is the largest prehistoric hilltop enclosure in North America.

geometric designs. The petroglyphs found were carved into sandstone and almost all were in hilly areas or along streams. A few were created in dolomite or limestone. Of the sixty-five, thirty-five are acceptable, Swauger stated, as Native American in origin and twenty-four are Euro-American. The few others are deemed as "uncertain."

Swauger also stated, "The Petroglyphs were carved by Algonquian speakers Late Prehistoric Period, likely proto-Shawnee, people living in Ohio sometime between A.D. 1200–1750. These people shared a set of symbols and perhaps mystic concepts with Ojibwa and other groups, chiefly Algonquian speakers."

Petroglyphs include:

Fairfield County: Kettle Hill Cave Petroglyph Site in Berne Township is about 1.64 miles west of Emery Cemetery. This area was once a hiding place for outlaws during the early years of the county. The block of Black Hand Sandstone is in storage at the Ohio History Connection in Columbus.

Erie County: Kelleys Island Petroglyph Site is also known as Inscription Rock. It is located just east of the ferry landing slip on the south shore of Kelleys Island. Among other things, it includes an image of a long-stemmed pipe.

Hocking County: Ash Cave Petroglyph Site is in the Hocking State Forest in Benton Township. A bird carved into Black Hand Sandstone is believed to be a Euro-American carving.

Jackson County: The Leo Petroglyph State Memorial is located at 357 Township Hwy 224 in Ray, Ohio, 45672. This sandstone petroglyph contains thirty-seven incredible images of humans and animals believed to have been created by the Fort Ancient Culture. The large flat sandstone sits on a hillside above a steep gorge.

Licking County: Newark Track Rock Petroglyph is in the Licking County Historical Museum in Newark. It was originally carved into Black Hand Sandstone on a vertical rock space about six miles west of Newark.

Lucas County: Turkey Foot Rock Petroglyph is in the Fallen Timbers Memorial Park in Monclova Township. It was once at the foot of the rapids at Maumee City at Presque Isle Hill.

Additional Information

The Ohio History Connection in Columbus, Ohio has one of the best collections of prehistoric artifacts in North America. It is located on the grounds of the Ohio Expo Center and State Fair at I-71 and 17th Ave. (Exit 111) in Columbus.

An Ohio Historical Marker entitled "Prehistoric Circular Earthworks" stands at 149 E. Franklin St. in Circleville next to the Circleville Municipal Court. Circleville derives its name from the circular portion of an 1,100-foot diameter Hopewell-era earthwork upon which the town was built. Town Director Daniel Dreisbach plotted the town atop the earthwork. An octagonal courthouse stood directly in the center.

An Ohio Historical Marker stands at Campbell Memorial Park dedicated to the Adena-era Shrum Mound along the west side of McKinley Ave. on Columbus's west side.

A marker entitled "Native Americans" stands near the intersection of Long St. and Neil Ave. in Columbus. It is dedicated to the mound builders and states that an estimated 200 burial and ceremonial mounds were once in Franklin County.

3
Rivers and Trails

For reasons that are still a mystery to archaeologists, the Fort Ancient people vanished from southern Ohio in the mid-to-late 17th century about the same time the first Europeans were entering Lake Erie territory. There is a generally obscure Shawnee tradition that says they are the heirs of the Fort Ancient culture. Meanwhile, a confederation of five Iroquois-speaking Indian tribes entered Ohio country and fought for dominance in the hunt for fur-bearing animals used for trade with English and Dutch merchants in the East. This came to be known as the Beaver Wars. Several tribes aligned with the French, including the Erie, Huron, and Shawnee, withdrew their alliance with the Iroquois and went into exile. The French were incensed at the invasion and destroyed Iroquois villages and crops, causing massive starvation. The Beaver Wars ended with the Treaty of Grande Paix (Great Peace) in 1701.

The setting was perfect for the next generation of Native Americans to return to Ohio country around 1720. The history of what passed for "roads" themselves is interesting. Mastodons once trampled though Ohio country searching for water and grass lands. Evidence of their existence is compelling. A complete mastodon skeleton, known as the Conway Mastodon, is on display at the Ohio History Center in Columbus. This fossil was discovered in 1887 in a swamp between Champaign and Clark counties.

Other proof was found in Grove City, Ohio in 1888 or 1889 when men digging in a tile pit between Columbus Street and a creek called Republican Run found a mastodon skeleton in the area behind St. John's Evangelical Lutheran Church. The whereabouts of this skeleton is unknown. In Columbus, a tooth from a mastodon was found on Dennison Ave. Mastodons were known to have several sets of teeth during their lifespans. In addition, nine remains of mastodons have been discovered in Pickaway County. Other fossils from the Ice Age in Franklin County include those of a giant beaver and three Ice Age horses.

After mastodons came the buffalo. As these 2,000-pound beasts entered Ohio country they wore deep paths in the soil as they reached grazing grounds. Early explorers called them "buffalo traces." Most of the trails were treacherous and impassible. There were no dams, no canals, and the swamps were not drained. Most of the trails were unmarked and bridges were rare.

Native Americans followed these traces and eventually paths like the *Scioto Trail* were forged. The *Scioto Trail* developed into the "Great Highway of the Shawnee" or "Warriors' Path" as it formed in the hunting grounds of northern Kentucky then headed north across the Ohio River at Lower Shawnee Town (now Portsmouth). The trail then passed the view of Mount Logan in Ross County—a scene that was later depicted on the Seal of Ohio. North of Chillicothe, it headed into the soft hills of the Pickaway Plains, once a prairie, and passed Maguck, a Delaware Indian village. This land was fertile farmland and home to many Native Americans, especially the Shawnee.

As the route headed further north to (now) Columbus, there were several Indian villages near the confluence of the Scioto and Olentangy rivers, including at least three Seneca-Mingo villages (collectively called Salt Lick Town). From the confluence of the Scioto and Olentangy, the trail headed up the Olentangy past the (now) city of Delaware and further north/northwest until it reached Wyandot villages in Wyandot County along the Sandusky River. From there the trail headed to Sandusky Bay and the fishing grounds of Lake Erie. U.S. Route 23 essentially follows most of this path.

At the city of Delaware in Delaware County there was a second junction of another major pathway, the *Cuyahoga War Trail*. This route headed northeast across what are today's cities of Fredericktown, Perrysville, Wooster, Loudenville, and Barberton to the west of Akron where it met the *Muskingum Trail*.

In central Ohio, a trail ran from Franklinton (Columbus) to Old Chillicothe, also called Old Town, near Xenia (Greene County). This trail, later to be called *Chenoweth's Trace*, passed through the village of Georgesville (Franklin County). Thomas and Elijah Chenoweth, brothers from Maryland, were the first settlers along Darby Creek

 Scioto Trail. The Scioto Trail ran from northern Kentucky to Sandusky Bay and connected the Shawnee's hunting grounds with Lake Erie.

near the village of Harrisburg in 1799, having purchased 200 acres from Franklinton founder Lucas Sullivant. They used this trail. In addition, two other trails passed through Madison County heading west to access villages on the Mad River.

A pathway known as *Old Indian Trail* was used by Tecumseh on his travels. The trail began east of (now) Plain City and headed west. That same trail was later used by the Pony Express. In 1809 pioneer Richard Taylor cleared the ground and it became Post Road (State Rt. 161).

The *Muskingum Trail* started at Ohio country's first settlement, Marietta, and ran along steep ravines to today's Stockport, Duncan Falls, Zanesville, Newcomerstown, Gnadenhutten, New Schoenbrunn, and Massillion to Summit Lake.

The *Miami Trail* in western Ohio country ran from the Ohio River at Cincinnati to (today's) Mason, Lebanon, Dayton, Troy, and Piqua to Fort Loramie and on to St. Marys. This area was like a modern highway interchange where a portage could lead travelers further north, east, or west by foot or canoe. The east sides of both the Great and Little Miami rivers were used constantly by hunters.

The *Shawnee-Miami Trail* began at the Scioto Trail at Maguck and headed northwest to London. From there it headed to Urbana, crossed the Mad River, and on to the Miami village of Pickawinnany.

The *Coshocton Trail* followed an old trace from the Shawnee capital at Circleville to Coshocton where the Delaware lived. Later, a part of it became portion of the National Road (US Rt. 40). It ran through (now) Amanda, Lancaster, Pleasantville, Thornville, Frazeyburg, and Wakatomuka to the Forks of the Muskingum.

Another trail, known as the *Great Trail,* was the most important east-west footpath in Ohio country. Originally blazed by Algonquian and Iroquois-speaking people as a path to Lake Erie, it ran west from Fort Pitt at the forks of the Ohio River to Fort Laurens, Fort Sandusky, and Fort Detroit.

But beyond the trails, of greater importance were Ohio's rivers. Generally, the rivers, except for the Ohio, ran north and south whereas the trails ran east and west. Three major river systems were immensely popular with Ohio's Native Americans. They are the Scioto, the Great Miami, and the Muskingum. Though the Great Miami was a superhighway for the Miami tribe and the Muskingum likewise for the Delaware, the Scioto was major transportation artery for all tribes traveling to numerous war expeditions against tribes south of the Ohio River.

Darby Creek. The Big Darby Creek runs 84 miles from its source near the Champaign/Union County line to Madison County. It is a tributary to the Lower Scioto River.

The Scioto River flows about 230 miles from its headwaters in Auglaize County through central Ohio to Portsmouth. It was possible for a Native American to travel from Lake Erie to the Ohio River via the Scioto by first using the Sandusky River to a short portage in Crawford County then heading down past the confluence of the Olentangy River in Columbus and on south.

The Scioto (a Shawnee word for "deer") runs north/south through the very heart of Ohio country and thus its significance in history should not be shortchanged. The Scioto was well suited for canoes and the rolling highlands east of the Little Miami River Valley made it easy for travelers to hike to either the Sandusky or Scioto rivers. These lands became home to the Shawnee and Delaware.

In 1757, a Virginian named James Smith is credited with being the first person to write a description of the Scioto saying that the timber near its banks was first rate. "There is ash, sugar trees, walnut, locust, oak and beech," he wrote.

The St. Marys River was a major route from its portages either to the Auglaize or to the two Miamis. The Great and Little Miami tributaries parallel until they both enter the Ohio River. The long glacial ridges along the area provided extra protection in bad weather. Soon pack horse trains would find the most hospitable route from Canada to the French colony of Louisiana through the Miami Valley and down to the Ohio River.

Almost the entire northwest quadrant of Ohio country was swampland within an area forty miles wide and 120 miles long. Though the only way to pass through this spongy marsh was by canoe, the territory provided excellent game hunting.

Of major significance was the Ohio River. Ohio is an Iroquois word for "Good River." Thomas Jefferson once said, "The Ohio is the most beautiful river on earth." The French called it "La Belle Riviere." The land on both sides of the river was rich with game and competing tribes from both the north and south of it fought for domination. Hundreds of early pioneers would brave this river in flat boats from Pittsburg to make the 981-mile trip west to Cairo, Illinois, where it empties into the Mississippi. Surveyors George Washington and William Crawford took a canoe from Pittsburgh to Mingo Bottom and explored Ohio in 1767. The river town of Marietta was founded in 1788 as Ohio's first settlement by the Ohio Company of Virginia. Some of the investors were members of Washington's family.

In central Ohio, the Big Darby Creek flows about eighty-four miles from its source in Logan, Champaign, and Union counties southeast to Circleville on the Scioto River in Pickaway County. The original name for the Big Darby was "Ollentangy" but was changed by early surveyors around 1796. The pioneer Jonathan Alder said the Big Darby was once called Crawfish Creek and the Little Darby was called Sycamore Creek. In addition, the river we now call the Olentangy was once called Whetstone Creek but renamed in 1833. The Big Walnut Creek was once nicknamed "Big Belly" and changed to Gahanna which was the Native American word for "three into one"— the confluence of Alum, Blacklick, and Big Walnut Creeks. Alum Creek was known by the Native Americans as "Seeklic-Sepung" or Salt Lick Creek. The Delaware, especially, liked to camp along Alum Creek. At the confluence today is Three Creeks Metro Park.

Of more importance as a source of salt for the Native Americans was a salt lick located in Jackson and Ross Counties at the confluence of the Scioto River and Scippo Creek. The Scioto Salt Lick is located about twelve miles south of (now) Chillicothe was a place used by many tribes to boil down salt and take it back to their home villages.

Ohio's geographic location made it a desirable destination for adventurous colonials. To the east was the Pennsylvania colony founded by William Penn. Penn was issued a land grant by King Charles II mostly due to a debt owed to Penn's father, Sir William Penn, a British admiral and politician. The translation of the word Pennsylvania is "Penn's Woods." To the south was the Virginia colony founded in 1607 by John Smith and other colonists. It was the first of the thirteen original colonies. To the north was a fort and settlement founded in 1701 by French trader Antoine de la Mothe Cadillac which he called Fort Pontchartrain du Detroit. The French word for Detroit is "strait." To the west was Indiana Territory which was sparsely populated by Native Americans. The name Indiana is generally thought to mean "Land of the Indians." The first settlement was Clarksville named after surveyor and soldier George Rogers Clark.

The sixty years between 1754 and 1814 would become the most hostile in Ohio history. The Native Americans would defiantly defend their lands as Anglo Americans entered and desired to make the territory their own. Men such as George Washington wanted to acquire Indian country to expand the new nation and to "civilize it." The Native Americans stood their ground as a "free people" and demanded that settlers be expelled.

The rivers and trails would become the bloody intersections of those opposing forces.

➤ Additional Information

An Ohio Historical Marker entitled "Scioto Trail" stands along the east side of the Olentangy River on Dublin Road south of Lane Road The marker states that the trail extends from the mouth of the Scioto River at Portsmouth and connects Shawnee hunting grounds in Kentucky with Lake Erie.

A historical marker entitled "Scioto River" sits at the west end of the Broad Street bridge on the Scioto River. It states that a wooden toll bridge was built across the water by Columbus's founder Lucas Sullivant in 1816. The marker was erected by the Federal Highway Administration, Ohio State Historical Preservation Office, and the Advisory Council on Historic Preservation.

A marker entitled "Old Indian Trail" stands east of Plain City at the intersection of Post Road (State Rt. 161) and Old 161 (County Rt. 308). It states that the trail was blazed by Tecumseh and later used by the Pony Express. It was erected by the Ohio Society of Daughters of American Colonists in 1941.

4
Mythology and Customs

The years between 12,000 B.C. and A.D. 1650 are known as the "pre-contact" years, meaning Native Americans had not yet encountered Europeans who had come to North America. Archaeologists consider A.D. 1600 as the beginning of the Historic Period when Native Americans first met European traders.

The Native Americans did not have a written language, but some believe they had an early form of writing in pictographs. Words, phrases, and especially creatures of nature were carved or painted onto sticks or plaques. Walum Olum, or "Red Record," is believed by some to be an account of the Delaware-Lenape's origin and migration painted onto sticks. Many modern scholars believe this to be a hoax created by scholar Constantine Rafinesque in the 19th century. Discussion on this topic is ongoing. Nevertheless, it was not until French and British fur trappers and traders made contact with the tribes that anything was written about them. Oral histories helped to carry the knowledge. It was then that the stories started to emerge about Indian mythology.

Mythology

Eastern Woodland Indians in Ohio country believed that they were in mystical harmony with nature and that every living thing had a soul or spirit. The Algonquian believed in "Gitchie Manitou" or "Wishemenetoo" (Great Spirit) who had moral authority among them and was believed to be a deity. Manitou was a supernatural being who controlled nature and was omnipresent. The Woodland Indians lived in a spirit-filled world which surrounded them in all aspects of their lives. They believed their human power came from a guardian spirit. The Shawnee, for example, believed that Aashaa Monetoo (Good Spirit) gave them their home along the Ohio River. Otshee Monetoo was the bad spirit. Bad spirits could be anywhere. The Native Americans believed illness was caused by bad spirits and would ask a medicine man, or healer, to call upon Manitou to cure the person. Certain tribal members had medicine bundles containing sacred objects such as bear claws to assist them in healing.

Mythology helped the Native Americans to explain the world to their children. Their ceremonies and rituals called upon the spirits to help them deal with the many struggles they faced every day. These spirits, they believed, were often formed in things such as animals, birds, or even rocks. Sometimes spirits were given human characteristics. Some believed animals could be transformed into humans and vice versa. This was an internal part of their daily lives.

The Eastern Woodland Indians were fascinated with the sky. The sky was where the knowledge for planting, seasons, and calendars came from. The moon, stars, and comets held a special place in their hearts, and many thought they were deities. The sun was especially important because they believed it was the Master of Life. Many tribes believed the Big Dipper was particularly important and they used several stories to explain its origin in the constellation. One such story is that the Big Dipper—Ursa Major (Great Bear or Great She-Bear) runs on all four legs across the heavens. Some believed the Aurora Borealis (Northern Lights) are spirits of the dead.

The Seneca believed that a meteor in the sky was a fire dragon. The stars had special powers, as did comets. The sun was generally depicted as a man and the moon a woman. The moon was very mysterious because it changed shape. A solar eclipse was an incredibly special supernatural event that some saw as a bad omen. Birds of the air were important. Thunderbirds held a special place in the hearts of Native Americans such as the Seneca. They believed a Thunderbird is a large mythological creature (a Nenimkee or Binesi) who created thunder by beating his wings. Lightning is produced by flashing his eyes.

Certain Ohio tribes believed animals had mystical powers. Coyotes were depicted in many stories and were believed to be tricksters who were companions with wolves, porcupines, and foxes. Rabbits and raccoons were also tricksters.

The Native Americans searched for powers from their guardian spirits, often heading alone into a forest or on top of a mountain to fast and meditate. The Iroquois, for example, found spirits in trees which they believed to be under the leadership of the Great False Face. While in these situations, and others, they believed the four winds could come as "truth bearers." The Ojibwa word for north wind was "Kiwetin" which would bring misfortune.

Indians believed that they had a constant struggle between good and evil and that evil spirits were everywhere. Delaware-Lenape and the Munsee believed Matanto were evil spirits. The devil had many names and masks were created in their image. Sorcerers and witches also used their power to do evil deeds. The Shawnee believed a 'cyclone person' was evil and that gruesome creatures associated with these creatures came in many shapes. These evil sources were different from medicine people and shamans, although some anthropologists believe that shamans are the basis of most magicians or sorcerers in folklore.

Shamans were medicine people (either men or women) who could achieve an altered state of consciousness (or trance) to interact with spirits who would assist them in healing. Herbs were immensely helpful in the process of healing. The shamans were more like religious figures who acted like mediums between the spirit world and the natural world. The Seneca, for example, believed malevolent forces caused pain. The Seneca also believed a corn and squash mixture could cure wounds. Many thought that illness was a sign of disorder in the community and that a "thunderer" was an immensely powerful medical healer. Sometimes songs were sung as medicine in healing rites.

Feasts were an intricate part of culture. They were performed mainly in honor of the spirits of the dead. Food was prepared and someone would address the spirits and say the meal was set out to honor them. At some later time, the living relatives would come and eat this feast. The Huron held a Feast of the Dead whenever a large village moved to another location so the souls of those who died could travel west. One year after the date of death, the Shawnee, for example, would perform a "Turning Dance" to honor the dead. They believed the dead had many forms. Some thought an owl would foretell death.

Masks were an important part of Native American life. Masks were used in religious and shaman rituals, initiation ceremonies, and war rituals. Scary masks were supposed to scare evil spirits out of the person. They were also given as gifts or used for entertainment purposes. The eagle was the most powerful mask and could only

 Wolf. *The wolf is a totem for the Seneca, Miami, Wyandot, Delaware, and Shawnee tribes. Totems are considered sacred objects or emblems of a tribe.*

be worn by a chief. Native Americans believed the person wearing a mask was taken over by a spirit and became the spirit represented by the mask. In healing rituals, they were used to summon the spirit world.

Many believed the underworld was beneath the soil from which humans emerged and to which humans returned. Evil creatures also lived there. Shamans were known to try and speak to the dead—what today we would call the "black arts." Some believed in magic that was performed by witches or sorcerers. It was believed that some members of a tribe saw visions and could communicate with the spiritual world. Sometimes the visions would be seen by an individual during dancing rituals.

Bears had an important place in Indian mythology. Some believed bears had both masculine and feminine energy. Bears represented the cycle of birth, death, and rebirth. Bears were also a symbol of leadership, strength, and wisdom. Several ceremonies revolved around bears. The Delaware had a 10-day winter event called the Bear Ceremony that was performed to strengthen the community.

The Native Americans had many different dances but the Green Corn Dance was a particularly important rite held in July or August when the crops matured. They believed that this was the beginning of a new year. This ritual would often last four to six days and many tribes would gather. The council of women would select the names of children born during the year and the chiefs would proclaim those names to those assembled. Another important event held in the fall, the Bread Dance, celebrated the harvest.

An annual twelve-day event, known as the Big House Ceremony, was held by the Delaware, Munsee, and Shawnee tribes. Here they held a religious ceremony where they worshipped Manitou, the protector of all animals in the forest. They carved a spirit face or mask, called Mising, on posts and held religious ceremonies where they worshipped Manitou.

Fire handlers were men who used fire to interpret dreams. Some of those who interpreted dreams were thought to communicate with the spiritual world. Fire's relationship to the sun made it incredibly special. Some tribes believed a cultural hero once made a perilous trip to steal fire so it could be used by human beings. Another aspect of fire says its light represents full achievement of creation.

Customs

Customs for Native American men and women were broken down by gender.

Men

Into the mix of mythology in their daily lives, the Woodland Indians had many customs. Many men had tattoos and plucked their hair except at the crown of their heads. They wore doeskin shirts and buckskin leggings. Some wore ponchos and some carried shoulder bags, but all wore moccasins. Every man had a blanket that was used not only to keep himself warm in bad weather but used to carry tools and other items. Sometimes the blankets were worn as a ceremonial dress. When available, men purchased flintlock horse pistols usually from merchants in Detroit where they could buy other supplies.

Men would chew a combination of dried tobacco, sumac, willow, and dogwood called Kinni Kinnick. They often traveled in birch bark canoes. To add sweetness to their food, they made sugar from the sap of maple trees.

Hunting was an important part of a boy's education around age fifteen. There was strict etiquette applied which meant trapping season was followed by the winter hunt. When the animals were brought back to camp, the meat was cut and placed on the roof of their huts or cabins to dry. Other lessons taught included how to catch raccoons, the frog life cycle, and how to imitate the calls of animals to lure them close for the kill.

War parties were a major part of Native American life. Men would fast before a battle to purify themselves. When it came time to retire for the night, they would create a large fire and sleep with their feet towards it. Fire was important for another reason—smoke was thought to carry messages to the Great Spirit.

War councils would be called. War chiefs were often younger men who had proven themselves. When a captive was taken hostage, his face was painted black—the mark of death. Warriors were thought by some to have magical powers.

Shamans were high officials in a tribe. Every camp had a shaman who was held in high regard for their support with the spirits.

Men and Women

The Shawnee had a bifurcated political system of various war and peace chiefs from local villages. Some women were given the position of peace chiefs. They had their own laws and there were consequences for breaking them. One could be accused of treason for revealing secrets of the medicine preparations as well as giving information to the enemy. If convicted, the person was put to death.

Horses were particularly important not only for travel but for trade. Men rode bareback and women often used buckskin saddles with a horn.

The Shawnee lived in rectangular lodges or wigwams due to the space being roomier. Wigwams were about ten feet in diameter and constructed from saplings angled to make a frame. Many were covered with bark or animal skins. Teepees were mostly used during hunting season because they were easier to move as hunters roamed through the woods hunting deer. Kentucky and Virginia were considered sacred hunting grounds.

Villages were small and typically numbered only a few hundred people or less. Many villages had a council house which was ninety feet long and thirty feet wide. Tribal councils would meet here. Sometimes there would be conflicts between war chiefs and peace chiefs. Native Americans believed in both justice and revenge. Many ceremonies were conducted in the council house or Big House, as it was called. For the Shawnee, many of the decisions were made by the entire tribe. When disagreements were settled between tribes, a calumet, a "pipe of peace," was passed around. Seneca women, unlike other tribes, had the power to veto a council's decision.

Both men and women loved jewelry. Hematite was found in both Muskingum and Morgan counties in Ohio and flint was found in Licking County. Many necklaces and bracelets were made from these materials. The Shawnee also wore ear spools and gorgets.

Wampum were shell beads gathered by tribes and strung together by tribal members. These items were used as presents, trade, or as important offerings in treaties. Legend says that the custom started with shamans who smoked a pipe. After they inhaled the smoke, beads would drop from their mouths.

Women and Children

Native American women wore blouses and skirts in the summer and leggings underneath in the winter. Some Native Americans wore hats, especially for ceremonies. The Shawnee had two female chiefs. One was a peace chief who supervised the planting and preparing of feasts and a war chief who was responsible for preparation of meat. The women were responsible for planting and gardening. Especially important was the planting of the "Three Sisters"—corn, beans, and squash. Corn, besides being a real staple, was used to provide a place for the beans to climb. The beans provided nitrogen to the soil. The squash helped to keep down the weeds. Women and children worked together to harvest the crops and pick such things as gooseberries, herbs, mandrakes, sunflower seeds, and ginger. In some parts of Ohio country were cranberry bogs. All these items helped keep them alive during the bare winter months.

Women also performed a lot of the back-breaking work of cutting and carrying wood. They gathered water and cooked most of the food—making spoons out of bison horns. As the men killed deer, buffalo, and elk for food, women dried their skins and stretched them before packing the items to sell to both French and British traders.

The Seneca women owned property and had political power. The heads of families and the bloodlines were traced through the mother. For women, gossip was often considered a crime. All Seneca, however, thought hospitality was important.

In Shawnee tribes, marriages were usually arranged by the parents. Girls married at age thirteen or fourteen and boys around age seventeen.

Hawk. The hawk is a totem for the Seneca, Wyandot, and Shawnee tribes.

The infant mortality rate was high among the Native Americans so particular care was taken with children. Small children were often put in hammocks, or baby swings, made with blankets tied to two trees or poles. These same infants were sometimes strapped to a cradle board until they could sit alone. Newborns were often bathed in cold water or dipped in streams to embolden them. Older children had few toys except for corn husk dolls made from corn stalks. They played games among themselves, many of which involved running. They also played stick ball and a form of ring toss. Many would conduct races with their ponies. Children were taught that bad behavior would bring sadness and that good conduct would earn rewards. Honesty and good character were prized.

Clans

Many Native American tribes inherited membership in a clan. Each clan was named after an animal (see list below).

For the Shawnee, the word 'Chillicothe' meant the name of a clan and is derived from the term for the village—the "principal place"—where the tribal leader lived. Once that leader died, another leader would be chosen, and his village would be named Chillicothe. For example, there were at least five villages in Ohio country that were once named Chillicothe. The locations of those villages were: Piqua (Pickawillany), Westfall, Xenia (Old Town), Frankfort, and Hopeton (three miles north of today's Chillicothe).

The following is a list of **Totems**—a group of animals symbolizing a clan or family:

Seneca: Beaver, wolf, bear, turtle, deer, hawk, heron.

Miami: Wolf, eagle, panther, turkey, and raccoon.

Wyandot: Turtle, wolf, bear, porcupine, beaver, deer, hawk, snake.

Delaware: Wolf, bear, dog, opossum, turtle, crane, chicken.

Shawnee: Wolf, bear, panther, owl, hawk, turkey, deer, raccoon, turtle, snake, horse, rabbit.

5
Chiefs and Sachems

The largest group of Native Americans in the central and southern regions of Ohio country were the Shawnee followed by Seneca and Wyandots. The Delaware were basically concentrated in the eastern part of Ohio country and the Miami in the western portion. The Ottawa lived in northern Ohio territory.

The following chiefs were prominent inhabitants of Ohio country during the 18th and early 19th centuries. They are listed by tribe.

The Shawnee

The primary Shawnee domain was the Ohio Valley that included southern Ohio, the Kentucky territory, and parts of Virginia that is now West Virginia. Some historians believe the Shawnee may be descendants of the Fort Ancient culture. The chiefs of the five different clans were subordinate to the principal chief. His word was law. The other chiefs, however, ruled their own jurisdictions.

The Shawnee were divided into septs (clans) and membership was passed down by the father. Every Shawnee clan was named after an animal. The two most dominant septs were the Chalahgawtha (or Chillicothe) and the Thawegila. They oversaw all things political and all things affecting the whole tribe. All other chiefs were under their control and all succeeding principal chiefs of the Shawnee Nation had to come from them. The other three subordinate septs were the Kispokotha (warfare and preparation of warriors), Peckuwe (maintenance of order or duty and in charge of religious celebrations), and Maykujay (matters of health, medicine, and food). Their most important chiefs were:

Black Fish: second in command to Cornstalk. When Cornstalk was killed, Black Fish became his successor and principal chief of all Shawnees and led attacks into Kentucky.

Black Hoof: war chief who lived along the Scioto River in Pickaway Plains. He was allied with the French and was present at Gen. Edward Braddock's defeat at Fort Duquesne (later Fort Pitt). He also fought at the Battle of Fallen Timbers. Black Hoof helped to negotiate the Treaty of Greene Ville and encouraged the Shawnee to adopt the American's way of life by learning to farm. President Thomas Jefferson gave him a gold chain as a symbol of friendship between America and the Shawnee. It is rumored that he lived to be 100.

Black Snake (Shemeneto): principal war chief and member of the Kispoko clan. He was at the Battle of Point Pleasant and was made war chief upon the death of Tecumseh's father Pucksinwah. He was also a leader in the defeat of Col. William Crawford's army in 1782.

Blue Jacket (Weyapiersenwah): prominent war chief of the Maykujay sept. Successor to Moluntha and husband to Wabethe. He led the Shawnee in Lord Dunmore's War (1774) and defeated both Gen. Harmar (1790) and Gen. St. Clair (1791). However, Blue Jacket's confederacy was defeated at Fallen Timbers (1794).

Captain Johnnie: civil chief of the Shawnee. He was present at the signing of the Treaty of Fort Finney.

Cheeseekau: older brother of Tecumseh and The Prophet who served as a mentor to his siblings. Like his younger brothers, Cheeseekau fought with the British. He was killed while attacking a stockade in (now) Tennessee in 1788.

Colonel Lewis (Quitewepea): born in Pickaway Plains and later moved his tribe from Wapakoneta to west of the Mississippi River on land given to the Shawnee by the U.S. government. He later moved them south to Arkansas territory. At one time it is believed that he was the brother-in-law of pioneer Jonathan Alder.

Cornstalk (Keightughqua): leader of the Shawnee Nation just prior to the American Revolution and is considered the greatest chief of the Scioto Indians. Born in 1720, probably in Pennsylvania. His village was seven miles southeast of Circleville near Camp Charlotte. He led raiding parties into western Virginia hoping to drive the British away from Shawnee territory. He was also part of Pontiac's Rebellion in 1763. He and his son, Elinipsico, were murdered at Fort Randolph during a diplomatic mission in 1777.

 A memorial to Chief Cornstalk can be found in Logan Elm State Memorial Park along Congo Creek south of Circleville. The memorial is near the site of his village.

Kishkalwa: Shawnee war chief who became totally disgusted with Ohio country after the Battle of Point Pleasant and led his Thawegila tribal clan south around 1774. However, they missed their home and eventually returned in 1790 but remained peaceful.

Laulewasikau (later known as Tenskwatawa and The Prophet): brother of Tecumseh who became a force in his own right. While Tecumseh was away on a recruiting mission, he lost the Battle of Tippecanoe. In the aftermath, the tribe abandoned Prophetstown and Gen. Harrison's men burned it to the ground.

Moluntha: Grand Sachem of the Shawnee who fought at the Siege of Boonesborough in 1778 with the British. Brother-in-law of Chief Cornstalk. Signed the Great Miami Treaty (also known as the Treaty of Fort Finney) in 1786. He was the titular king of all Shawnees and had children by several wives, including Nonhelema. Moluntha was murdered at the age of ninety-four by an American soldier during Logan's Raid as he held a copy of the Treaty of Fort Finney in his hand. Frontiersman Simon Kenton witnessed his death.

Nonhelema: village chieftainess and female warrior known as the Grenadier Squaw of the Thawakila clan. Born circa 1722, she spoke four languages and often served as an interpreter. She was the sister of Cornstalk and Silverheels and grew to an imposing

 Crane. The Crane is the symbol for the Delaware tribe. Totem animals are creatures that represent a person, family or entire tribe.

six and a half feet tall. Known as a fierce warrior in her early years, she and her family lived on Scippo Creek in the Pickaway Plains next to her brother's village. She fought against Col. Henry Bouquet at the Battle of Bushy Run in 1763 and in other battles. Over her lifetime, she was married to three Shawnee warriors and had an unknown number of children by other men. One of her paramours was British Indian agent Thomas McKee. They had a son together. In later years she sought peace while her fellow tribal members wanted war. She was made an outcast until she died at age sixty-six.

Pucksekaw (Jumper): fought against American scouts at Symmes Creek, Reeve's Crossing on Paint Creek, and Ohio Brush Creek. He was present at the Treaty of Greene Ville.

Pucksinwah: war chief and father of Tecumseh. He fought in and was killed at the Battle of Point Pleasant.

Red Pole: civil chief of the Shawnee Nation. Possibly a half-brother of Blue Jacket.

Sauwauseekau: brother of Tecumseh killed at the Battle of Fallen Timbers.

Tecumseh: warrior chief and political leader who organized a multi-tribal confederation to fight the Americans. Most likely born on the Mad River west of Springfield, his father was killed at the Battle of Point Pleasant during Lord Dunmore's War. He sided with the British in the War of 1812 in the siege of Detroit where his military brilliance helped the British to defeat the Americans in several battles. His brother, known as The Prophet, was the political and religious leader of the Shawnee. Tecumseh was shot and killed in a meadow alongside the Thames River in Ontario, Canada while fighting for the British in the War of 1812.

Yellow Hawk: successor to Black Snake.

Wasegoboah: brother-in-law of Tecumseh who died in the Battle of Thames.

The Delaware (Lenape) migrated from the Delaware Valley in the northeastern woodlands. Five of their great chiefs were:

Anderson (Kikthawenund): also known as Captain Anderson or William Anderson: born along the Susquehanna River in Pennsylvania at Anderson's Ferry and later moved to Ohio country. Anderson's father was of European ancestry and his mother was the daughter of a Delaware chief (of the Turkey clan). He signed the Treaty of Greene Ville in 1795 as chief of his clan and moved to (now) Anderson, Indiana. After the Battle of Tippecanoe (in which he did not participate), Gov. Harrison demanded that the Delaware return to Piqua, Ohio. Tecumseh tried to get him to participate in his confederacy, but he refused. After the War of 1812, Anderson's Town in Indiana was rebuilt and became the principal village of the Delaware. In 1821, Chief Anderson led about 800 of his people to Kaskaskia, Illinois and then to a new home in southwest Missouri. In 1830, he moved them further west to a reserve in the Kansas Territory where he died around age seventy-six.

Buckongahelas: Lenape Delaware war leader. Fought in the French & Indian War. Ally of the British during the Revolutionary War and attacked Wheeling during the First Siege of Fort Henry in 1777. He later lived among the Ottawa and fought against Gen. Harmar, Gen. St. Clair, and Gen. Wayne but signed the Treaty of Greene Ville and other treaties until his death in 1804 at the age of nearly 100.

Captain Pipe: Delaware tribal chief whose nickname was Hobocan, "tobacco pipe," and whose real name was Konieschquanoheel. Fought in Pontiac's War in 1763. He was the principal captain of the Wolf tribe of the Delaware. In 1782, he participated in Col. William Crawford's defeat and may have been the one to mark Crawford for death. Some historians think it was Capt. Pipe who threatened to kill Simon Girty if he intervened in Crawford's behalf.

White Eyes (Koquechagachton): war chief who was speaker of the Delaware Head Council. He became a mediator in negotiating treaties.

Wingenund: war chief whose town of Tuscarawa Indians was about six miles from Coshocton, Ohio. Wingenund moved his people to (now) Wyandot County in 1781 due to threats by soldiers from Fort Pitt. About 100 starving Indians returned in February 1782 to the Gnadenhutten/Salem area to harvest their corn with the intent of returning to Wyandot County. All but a few were massacred by soldiers under the command of Col. David Williamson from Fort Pitt.

The Huron

This tribe was close to the Wyandots and some historians say they are the same.

The Miami

The Miamis were once the most powerful tribe in Ohio country who settled among the Shawnees and Delawares. All three, plus the Ottawas, spoke an Algonquian dialect. Three of their important chiefs were:

Le Gris: an important Eel River Miami chief.

Little Turtle (Michikinikwa): has been referred to as the Miami's greatest war chief who defeated the forces of both Gen. Harmar and Gen. St. Clair. He was elected to the supreme command of the united war parties. He was born on the Eel River in the Indiana territory in 1747—his father was a Miami chieftain and his mother was Mohican. He was known as a great orator and was present at the Treaty of Greene Ville. He died in Fort Wayne.

Pacanne: influential chief who lived between the Maumee and Wabash rivers. He mostly sided with the British and his family controlled the 8-mile strip of land known as the Long Portage used by traders traveling between Canada and Louisiana. He worked with Le Gris and Little Turtle but refused to sign the Treaty of Greene Ville. Instead, he sent his nephew Chief Richardville.

The Ottawa

This tribe moved to northern Ohio from southern Ontario and the Michigan territory around 1740. They fought for the British during the American Revolution. Several chiefs stand out above the others:

Egushawa: war chief who became principal chief and successor to Pontiac. In 1778, he led the fight to recapture Vincennes with British Lt. Gov. Henry Hamilton's expedition. He helped to defeat both Gen. Josiah Harmar and Gen. Arthur St. Clair and fought a losing battle against Gen. Anthony Wayne. He became a key spokesman for the Ojibwa, Potawatomi, and Wyandot tribes and negotiated the Treaty of Greene Ville. His name means "The Gatherer."

Negig (Little Otter): attacked Gen. Anthony Wayne on October 16, 1793, killing 30 soldiers and capturing others.

Oquanoxa (Ocquinoxcy): led the last war party to Fort Wayne to avenge the death of a fellow tribesman in 1824.

Otusse: this son of Pontiac fought against the Americans during the War of 1812, helping to defeat them along the River Raisin near Detroit in January, 1813.

Pontiac: war chief in the 1760s related to the Miamis. Together with the Shawnee, Wyandots, Delawares, Miamis, and Seneca, they called themselves the "Five Nations of Scioto" and fought as a considerable obstacle to Britain's expansion. Pontiac was probably born in the Maumee River Valley and became a great leader. A Frenchman once wrote down a vision of Pontiac's that is known as "Pontiac's Manuscript." Pontiac had hoped for peace under an Indian confederacy that opposed English outsiders on Native lands. He was assassinated near the French town of Cahokia, Illinois in 1769.

Wauseon: chief who held the last council with the U.S. government to convey Ottawa lands to the government before leaving Ohio. Chief Waseon (the 'u' was added later) was the brother of Ottokkee. He was tall and a good speaker who led his people's exodus to Kansas. His name means "far away."

The Seneca (also called Mingo)

Seneca-Cayuga were an Iroquoian-speaking people who migrated west to Ohio country and mostly settled among the Shawnees and Delawares. Some of their greatest chiefs were:

Cornplanter: chief of the Seneca tribe who sided with the English during the Revolutionary War. In 1801 he met with President Thomas Jefferson and won a land

Turtle. The turtle is a symbol for the Wyandot, Delaware, and Shawnee tribes.

grant in Pennsylvania for his people. He then supported the American side in the War of 1812. He died in 1836 at the age of 104.

Guyasuta (Kiasutha): born in 1720 in western New York, Guyasuta became the premiere leader of the Iroquois Confederacy in the Ohio Valley. In 1755, he fought for the French against the British and their colonial militiamen allies. When Fort Quebec fell to the British in 1759, Canada became a British colony and the tribes had to make peace with them to get gun powder. He agreed to arrange the return of all Anglo captives taken during the war with the French. Within four years, Guyasuta felt the British were treating the tribes shamefully and sided with Chief Pontiac to oust them. He also was a mentor to a young captive named Simon Girty who later turned against his fellow Americans. Eventually Guyasuta joined a peace council.

Logan (Tachnechdorus or John Logan): a Cayuga war leader who, upon moving to Ohio country, became affiliated with the Seneca. He sought revenge for family members killed in the Yellow Creek Massacre in 1774. After Lord Dunmore's War he delivered "Logan's Lament," and sought a peace treaty. He was known as Logan the Orator.

Pluggy (Plukkemehnotee): an ally of Logan during Lord Dunmore's War. He was also allied with the British during both the French and Indian War and the American Revolution. He commanded raids against American settlements through-out Ohio country until his death in 1776. Pluggy's Town was located along the Olentangy River (now Delaware, Ohio) and was used by Wyandots, Ottawas, and Chippewas to stage raids.

Red Jacket (Otetiani, later Sagoyewatha): born in 1750 in Canoga, New York, he was chief of the Wolf clan. He, along with 28 other tribal chiefs, attended the Grand Council in the summer of 1792 at the confluence of the Auglaize and Maumee rivers (known as The Glaize). Aware that Gen. Anthony Wayne was building an army at Fort Pitt, this confederation of tribes wanted the Ohio River recognized as their boundary against trespassers (settlers). He was considered a great orator who sought to present himself as an enemy of Anglos but secretly signed property cessions to protect his dealings with Americans. Many Seneca considered him a coward, but he ultimately was able to remain a chief.

Succohanos: chief who became Jonathan Alder's adoptive father.

Wyandots, also spelled Wyandottes, were Iroquoian-speaking Indians from the eastern woodlands. The following Wyandot chiefs were most prominent:

Between-the-Logs: friend of the Americans who fought with Gen. Anthony Wayne at Fallen Timbers. He later became a licensed preacher with the Methodist Church.

Chief Darby: the man for whom the Big Darby and Little Darby Creeks are named. Both waterways are designated rivers. The village of Darbydale is also named for him.

Deunquod: chief who resisted Christianity.

Half King: principal chief and the highest dignitary of the Wyandots at Upper Sandusky. Of all the Indian allies of the British, the Wyandots were the most powerful.

Leatherlips (Shateyaronyah): was of the Porcupine Clan of the Wyandots, the same as his friend Chief Tarhe. He was also related to Roundhead. Leatherlips was well known for never breaking a promise. He signed the Treaty of Greene Ville which made certain Wyandots angry. In retaliation, the elderly chief was falsely accused of witchcraft and killed by his own tribal members in a village along the Scioto River. The spot of the assassination is about two miles north of Dublin, Ohio.

Mononcue: chief speaker of the Wyandot Nation. He was a noted orator who became a licensed preacher of the Methodist Church.

Roundhead: he signed the Treaty of Greene Ville and became a war chief under Tarhe until 1812 when he sided with the British and became a strong member of Tecumseh's Confederacy against the U.S. He was killed with Tecumseh at the Battle of the Thames.

Solomon, John (Shiawa): chief of the Wyandots who signed the Treaty of 1832 at McCutcheonsville in Crawford County, which sold a reservation of 16,000 acres to the U.S. government.

Summundewat: principal chief and historian for his tribe. Summundewat was a devout Methodist and gifted preacher with a commanding presence. In 1841 while on a winter hunting trip, he and his wife were murdered in Henry County by outlaws who stole their furs.

Tarhe (The Crane): Grand Sachem of the Wyandots. Born near Detroit to a mother who was of the Porcupine Clan. He was 6'4"—exceedingly large for a Native American. He served under Cornstalk and was a close friend of Seneca Chief Logan.

He fought against American generals Clark, Bouquet, Harmar, St. Clair, and Wayne and was believed to be the only chief to survive the Battle of Fallen Timbers. He then signed the Treaty of Greene Ville and sought peace. At the beginning of the War of 1812, he disagreed with Tecumseh and became an ally of the U.S. He was chief spokesman for the Native Americans at the Council of Franklinton (now Columbus) with Gen. William Henry Harrison. At age 72, he was at the Battle of the Thames in Canada when Tecumseh was killed. Tarhe lived in several different villages during his life, including one in Columbus. Toward the end of his life he returned to his village near (now) Upper Sandusky called Crane Town. His daughter, Myerrah (White Crane), married Isaac Zane, the founder of Zanesville, Ohio. Chief Tarhe died in Cranetown in 1818 at the age of seventy-six.

Walk-in-the-Water: a village chief in the Detroit area. At nearly six-feet tall, he was a fearless fighter who signed the Treaty of Greene Ville. He was considered extremely passionate in his vision for his people and often consulted with and supported Tarhe. During the War of 1812, he approached U.S. General William Hull about siding with the Americans. When he was rejected, he joined the British at Fort Walden and allied himself and his sixty warriors with Tecumseh.

> ### Additional Information

Note: Today there are three federally recognized Shawnee tribes divided into three groups: 1) Absentee Shawnee (those who moved to the Southwest), 2) Eastern Shawnee of Oklahoma (those who moved to Oklahoma and Missouri), and 3) Loyal Shawnee (those who went to Kansas).

Shawnee State University and Kent State University are involved in partnership with the Ohio tribes. The Shawnee are considered continually active in preserving their culture.

The Myaamia Center (Bonham House) at Miami University in Oxford, Ohio has a partnership with the Miami Tribe of Oklahoma. It serves as the research arm of the tribe's language and cultural revitalization efforts.

The Ohio State University offers an American Indian Studies minor at the Newark campus.

Chief Black Hoof Memorial is in St. John's Cemetery, Wapakoneta, Ohio.

There are two memorials to Chief Cornstalk—one in Tu-Endie-Wei State Park, Point Pleasant, West Virginia, and one in Logan Elm State Memorial Park near Circleville, Ohio.

The Chief Leatherlips Monument is at 7377 Riverside Dr., Dublin, Ohio.

The Chief Little Turtle Memorial is at 640 Lawton Pl., Fort Wayne, Indiana.

The Chief Logan Memorial is in Fort Hill Cemetery, Cayuga County, New York.

6

Ohio Indian Wars

Upon Ohio country in the mid-18th century lay a massive checkerboard of rough and tumble players moving around in an uncoordinated effort to conquer this rich new territory just beyond the Appalachian Mountains. So unknown was this mysterious land that people living in the original thirteen Colonies simply called it "the West."

To the east, the Colonies were full of British nationals who ran the government from their stronghold in Williamsburg, Virginia. They were aided by Loyalists born in the Colonies who believed in the British Crown. Royalists, or King's Men, came from all walks of life. These people were also called Tories. They believed that the Colonies should be ruled by a King or Queen.

Those on the opposing political side were called Patriots—native-born men and women who supported the Revolution and independence from Britain.

There were also French trappers and traders who did not want to settle land but only wanted to hunt along Ohio country lakes and rivers where they could make a living selling their furs. They were the ones who originally founded Detroit in 1701 as a fur trading post. At the time, the French had claimed Canada and called it "New France." In the mid-1700s, Pierre-Joseph Celeron di Bienville and 250 men were sent from Montreal in 1749 to explore the Ohio country and renew a friendship with the Native Americans. Celeron buried six metal plates along six tributaries of the Ohio River to mark France's presumed ownership. France claimed all of Ohio country.

At the same time, Britain claimed the Ohio Valley due to purchases of land from the Native Americans. After the French were defeated in the French and Indian War (1754–1763), the British made the Ohio country part of the borders of their Quebec colony.

Then there were Native Americans who roamed the land in a nomadic or semi-nomadic fashion with the men hunting and fishing and the women tilling soil to grow crops. Children assisted by foraging for nuts and berries. Basically, the major tribes were: Wyandot in Ohio's north-central and northwest areas, Delaware in the eastern portion, Miami in the western part, and Shawnee in the central and southern part of the Ohio territory. Other Indian nations roamed as well. All of them were ruled autonomously.

Many of the tribes in Ohio country traded with the French in places like Fort Detroit. The Wyandots, for one, fought for their French allies during the French and Indian War. When France lost, the British took over Fort Detroit. Some of the tribes, however, did not like the fact the British refused to leave. Chief Pontiac of the Ottawa tribe led his warriors against the British in an act now called Pontiac's Rebellion. Pontiac felt that France did not have the right to cede French claims to Indian land to the British. He boldly claimed that the Ottawa had never been conquered by any nation.

The British prevailed against the French but signed the Proclamation of 1763 recognizing the Native Americans' right to their own land and disallowing colonists from crossing the Ohio River. The line was declared that in October by King George III in the aftermath of Britain's victory in the French and Indian War. To the Native Americans' relief, it forbade all settlement west of a line along the Appalachian Mountains.

It did not take the Native Americans long to switch allegiance to Britain during the American Revolution. They liked trading with the British to obtain guns and assumed that if the Continental Army under Gen. George Washington prevailed, settlers would pour north across the Ohio River. They also hoped the British would keep settlers from crossing the Ohio River and into Indian territory.

Nothing encapsulates the discourse between Native Americans and frontier settlers more than an incident called the Yellow Creek Massacre in April 1774. The event was preceded by a militia raid, believed to be led by frontiersman (later Colonel) Michael Cresap, where a small group of Native Americans were murdered near the Ohio River. Some historians have argued that Cresap was not present at the event, although he led other raids during that time. On April 30, Daniel Greathouse and others murdered thirteen women and children, most of whom were family members of Seneca Chief Logan, also known as John Logan. This attack occurred at the mouth of Yellow Creek on the upper Ohio River near (now) New Cumberland, West Virginia. The murders were particularly egregious because one pregnant Indian woman was strung up by her wrists then impaled on a stake. Logan was enraged and led raids on settlers, scalping at least thirty men. (Logan would name Cresap, some say erroneously, in his famous speech known as "Logan's Lament.") The Yellow Creek Massacre is thought to be one of the causes a few months later of Lord Dunmore's War between the Colony of Virginia and the Shawnee/Seneca nations in Ohio country. (See Chapter 7 on the Battle of Point Pleasant.) This incident proved to be a predicate for the Revolutionary War in 1776.

After the Treaty of Paris in 1783 ended the American Revolution, Britain recognized the independence of the United States and ceded its land east of the Mississippi River. However, they retained possession of their Canadian lands. They also continued to trade guns and other goods with the Ohio tribes out of Fort Detroit and later British Fort Miamis in far northwest Ohio (now Toledo).

As the United States of America was born in the wake of the Treaty of Paris in 1783, the composition of the army had several components. At the start of the American Revolution, the army, for example, was a loose band of militia and citizen soldiers under the control of individual states. When Washington was put in command, they became more professional. The Minutemen of the American Revolution were civilian colonists organized into companies who were self-trained. They are best remembered for being ready at 'a minute's notice.'

The regular army was comprised of highly organized military men whereas the militia were loosely organized civilians who worked for free. They were often termed as "auxiliary" or "irregulars." The militia officers voted to select their commander.

A "levy" was a part-time soldier, also regular army, in a militia. A levy was generally recruited for a specific time for one particular need. They were often referred to as "green troops."

In the aftermath of the American Revolution, the Native Americans in the Ohio frontier were not about to capitulate to Gen. Washington and his victors. Starting in the 1780s until 1813 the confederacy of Ohio Indians fought to retain land they declared as their own. Turbulence reigned throughout Ohio country.

The lead into the Ohio Indian Wars, also known as the Northwest Indian Wars, essentially began with three treaties. The Treaty of Fort McIntosh was signed in 1785. The Wyandots, Delaware, Ottawa, and Ojibwa ceded most of Indian land in Ohio south of a line from Fort Laurens to the confluence of St. Marys and St. Joseph rivers (which forms the Maumee). It put the tribes who signed under the protection of the new United States government. In return, those tribes were to be given land in northwestern Ohio known as the Great Black Swamp. The Native American tribal representatives who signed the document were young and immature. They were given alcohol before the signing and were easily swayed.

The Shawnee and Miami refused to sign. They wanted to retain their land north of the Ohio River. The American government promised there would be no more settlers in Indian territory, but they soon broke their promise.

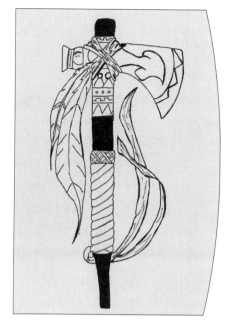

Tomahawk

On January 31, 1786, the Shawnee signed the Treaty of Fort Finney (also known as the Treaty at the Mouth of the Great Miami). They agreed to relinquish their land in southwest Ohio and southern Indiana and move to the Black Swamp. Still, many tribes disagreed.

Another major irritant to the Native Americans was the establishment of the Northwest Territory formed by the new U.S. government in 1787. The territory included present day Ohio, Indiana, Illinois, Michigan, and Wisconsin with its capital at Marietta (1788–1799) then Chillicothe (1799–1803). The Native Americans did not consent to it. Ohio would become the 17th state in the union in 1803 and the first one born from the Northwest Territories.

The American government next sent Gen. Arthur St. Clair, governor of the new territories, to meet with Native Americans at Fort Harmar in 1789. The proposed treaty reiterated the Treaty of Fort McIntosh in which the Native Indians would give up their land in southern and eastern Ohio. It also stipulated that soldiers would prevent squatters from settling on specific Indian reservations. St. Clair threatened the tribes if they did not sign but also offered a bribe in the form of $3,000 worth of gifts if they would do so. Several chiefs signed it, hoping to live in peace. The Shawnee, however, rejected the treaty and reminded St. Clair that the Ottawa, Wyandot, and Delaware did not speak for the entire confederacy. The treaty failed and the Shawnee went to Detroit to purchase more guns so they could attack settlers along the Ohio River.

The following events took place in what is known as the Ohio Indian Wars or the Northwest Indian Wars:

Gen. Harmar's Defeat—1790

In 1790, Secretary of War Henry Knox was thoroughly disgusted with the conflict in Ohio country and ordered Brevet Brig. Gen. Josiah Harmar, commander of the U.S. Army in the Northwest Territory, to attack the Native Americans as a "punitive expedition." Harmar was stationed at Fort Washington (now Cincinnati). He gathered 320 regular soldiers and about 1,100 Pennsylvania and Kentucky militiamen as his fighting force. The militiamen were poorly trained and mostly undisciplined. Nevertheless, Harmar left with the intent to attack Miami, Shawnee, and Delaware villages in western Ohio. Scouts for Chief Little Turtle of the Miami spotted the detachment led by Col. John Hardin.

The Native Americans had the advantage from the start. Primarily, they knew the land better than anyone—they were fighting on home territory. There were virtually no settlers in Ohio except for a few dotted along the Ohio River. Most of the trails used by the army were blazed by tribes on game hunting expeditions. Furthermore, they traveled light and fast which made them particularly dangerous. They could strike with surprise, then disappear without a trace. Most military historians would call these methods "guerilla tactics."

On October 19, Hardin sent a scouting party with the intent to attack the village of Chief Le Gris known as Kekionga (now Fort Wayne). The detachment was ambushed by Little Turtle's warriors in what is known as the Battle of Heller's Corners. At least 40 Americans were killed.

Harmar, himself, arrived at Kekionga on October 20 and sent 300 men under Ensign Phillip Hartshorn north to scout the Indians. Eight miles north they were ambushed and twenty of Hartshorn's men were killed. He retreated.

On October 22, Hardin, along with 300 militia and 60 regulars, spotted 1,000 Native Americans, including Little Turtle, Blue Jacket, and Le Gris, encamped at Kekionga. Hardin prepared his attack and expected Gen. Harmar and his men to cover his back. Some historians have surmised that Harmar was intoxicated at this point and became frightened. He and his men never arrived. Hardin moved forward with about sixty regulars and 300 militia.

In an action known as the Battle of Pumpkin Fields, Little Turtle attacked first. The militia gave chase and soon the regulars were isolated. Little Turtle attacked one detachment, killing many. A second detachment charged into a wooded area and was ambushed when Shawnee and Miami attacked from three sides. Hardin's men held for two hours, expecting reinforcements. When no help arrived, they retreated. The army lost 129 men and ninety-four wounded. The Native Americans lost at least 120 warriors.

Harmar ordered a retreat to Fort Washington. After his return, Harmar was accused of wrongdoing, including being drunk on duty. A court martial was conducted in 1791 but Harmar was exonerated of all charges.

To that point in history, Harmar's Defeat was the worst loss of U.S. forces at the hands of the Indian confederacy. President Washington was furious.

Battle of the Wabash—Gen. St. Clair's Defeat—1791

When word reached Knox that Gen. Harmar's army had been defeated, he, too, was furious. On March 21, 1791 he ordered Gen. St. Clair to attack the Shawnee and Miami along the Wabash River. To do that, Henry Knox demanded that St. Clair muster 3,000 men—a large army for what was considered a wilderness outpost.

St. Clair and his officers went to work to find 2,400 levies and militia from Pennsylvania and Kentucky to supplement his 600 regulars. The officers of the militia elected Gen. Richard Butler as their commander. St. Clair did not like him. Nevertheless, a plan was made to drive the Native Americans out of the Ohio country and open the way to drive the British out of Detroit.

The Native Americans had a network of spies constantly skulking the Ohio country for the military's movements. They also had three Americans—Simon Girty, Matthew Elliott, and Alexander McKee—who were Indian allies and served as translators and scouts.

The British in Detroit received word that a large American army was gathering at Fort Washington with plans to attack Shawnees and Miamis. The British sent arms and supplies to Little Turtle of the Miami and Blue Jacket of the Shawnee via the three renegade Americans. The British would not fight with the Native Americans because President Washington would have regarded that as an act of war. The Native Americans gathered warriors from most of their confederacy, including Wyandots, Delawares, Ottawas, and Potawatomis.

St. Clair's campaign was doomed from the start. In mid-September he sent men to construct a series of forts to serve as supply lines. The first of these was Fort Hamilton on the banks of the Great Miami River. St. Clair did not arrive there until October 1, 1791—late in the year to begin a wilderness campaign due to pending cold weather. Most of his men were untrained, unprofessional, and ill-equipped.

The weather turned bad and the supply lines failed. The cannons were difficult to drag through the rough terrain. St. Clair became ill with gout and was constantly in a sour mood. He continually argued over strategy matters with Butler. The militia soon became discouraged with St. Clair's leadership. They stopped to build a stockade called Fort Jefferson but supplies were still late. Things were moving at a snail's pace.

The men grew hungry and started to desert. To try and stop that action, St. Clair had three of them hanged in front of the army.

Nothing seemed to go right for the Americans. The army made extraordinarily little progress because supplies were so delayed. It was difficult to travel through the woods and the men were getting sick from the cold. Another sixty militiamen from Kentucky deserted *en masse*. Morale was horrible.

On November 3, the army regulars set up camp on the east side of the Wabash. A smaller group of militiamen was on the west bank. Little did St. Clair know that Girty was three miles away. By the morning of November 4, Little Turtle of the Miami and Blue Jacket of the Shawnee were ready to strike with Girty in command of the Wyandots.

The Native Americans opened fire and rushed the militia. Another group of warriors attacked the main camp. Little Turtle sent his men to outflank the regulars as the soldiers loaded their cannon. The cannon blasted into the air. Simon and the Wyandots continued to shoot with muskets and rifles. Within a short period of time, the members of the artillery crew were dead.

The battle raged and St. Clair coursed back and forth yelling orders. Before the battle was over, he had several horses shot out from under him. He called for a bayonet charge. The Wyandots ran into the woods with the Americans right after them. However, when they reached the trees, the tables turned. The two sides fought for three hours and the army suffered heavy casualties.

St. Clair ordered a retreat. The warriors chased them, killing and scalping several more men as they fled.

The Battle of the Wabash was the worst defeat inflicted on the U.S. Army by the Native Americans. Only twenty-four regulars were unscathed. Altogether 632 Americans died and 264 were wounded. Only twenty-one Native Americans were killed and forty wounded.

Congress placed a hefty reward for anyone who could catch Simon Girty.

Gen. Anthony Wayne and the Battle of Fallen Timbers—1793/94

President Washington realized after St. Clair's defeat that a well-trained regular army led by a strong commander was needed to defeat the fierce Ohio country Native Americans. He wanted a skilled leader to strengthen his army in the Northwest Territory and form it into a more competent and combatant fighting force. Washington wanted nothing less than to end the bloodshed in the region and make it more suitable to settlers.

On April 3, 1792, Washington selected retired Brig. Gen. Anthony Wayne to fill that task. Wayne proved himself an able commander during the American Revolution who demanded much needed discipline among his troops.

Wayne left for Fort Pitt knowing his assignment would be daunting. The Native Americans considered all settlers on the north side of the Ohio River to be trespassers. When they learned Wayne was in Pittsburgh, the Native Americans held four councils along the Auglaize River with twenty-eight tribes to strategize over the pending battle they knew was near. The Miamis, Shawnees, Wyandots, Ottawas, and Potawatomis declared they would fight if the Americans refused to recognize the Ohio River as the boundary, but they knew "Mad Anthony" would be a most worthy opponent.

The chiefs sent a letter to Congress discussing terms for peace. Henry Knox sent his reply in February, 1793. The Indians asked Simon Girty to translate it. Knox agreed to send delegates to meet with their chiefs, but Knox demanded they stop trading with the British. They agreed to meet in Upper Sandusky, a major Wyandot village, on June 1.

Meanwhile, Wayne was training his army in the methods of the bayonet charge while instilling strict discipline. By May he was ready to move his troops to Fort Washington from Pittsburgh to supplement the troops stationed there.

Not all Native Americans agreed with the strategy to fight. The Six Nations of the Iroquois Confederation under Joseph Brant plus the Ottawa, Ojibwa, and Potawatomi nations were willing to let American forts remain north of the Ohio River and move the boundary from the Ohio to the Muskingum River. The Shawnee, Miami, and their allies refused and had Alexander McKee write a formal letter to Knox stating the U.S. had no right to the Ohio country.

Knox took this as a declaration of war and set Wayne free to attack the Native Americans.

One of Wayne's first actions was to build Fort Greene Ville (Darke County) six miles north of Fort Jefferson where they made winter camp. He next sent infantrymen to the site of St. Clair's defeat to build Fort Recovery (Mercer County) to use as a staging area for his assault.

The British in Canada soon learned of Wayne's planned advance. Gov. Gen. Guy Carlton ordered a new military post called Fort Miamis (now Toledo) built on the Maumee River and garrison it with soldiers from Detroit. It was a direct violation of the peace treaty between Britain and the U.S., but Carlton wanted to prove he was in alliance with the Native Americans and urged them to unite. The tactic worked— Little Turtle and Blue Jacket collected a force of 1,200 men in their confederacy by mid-June. He also had British traders and Canadian frontiersmen ready to fight.

On June 30, 1794, 1,500 members of the Native American confederacy, led by Little Turtle, Blue Jacket, and Simon Girty, successfully attacked a supply train leaving Fort Recovery. The Native Americans killed fifteen soldiers and stole 300 horses. The next day the confederacy boldly attacked the fort but were decimated by cannon fire and forty Indians were killed. The soldiers held strong. The dejected Ottawas and Ojibwas headed home, but Girty pleaded with them to return and they reluctantly agreed. He surmised that if they could get Wayne's army out in the open, they could win as they had every such battle. Nonetheless, the confederacy was weakened.

In late July, Wayne ordered construction of Fort Defiance (now Defiance, Ohio) to use as a supply depot. The fort was so named because Kentucky militiaman Charles Scott said of the garrison, "I defy the English, Indians, and all the devils of hell to take it."

Little Turtle wanted peace and sought negotiations. Blue Jacket and Ottawa Chief Turkey Foot wanted to fight. Tribal leaders chose Fallen Timbers for their battle because Wayne's cavalry would have trouble advancing over trees toppled by a tornado. This time they would be aided by Canadian militiamen dressed like Native Americans.

By the day of the battle, August 20, the Indian confederacy had not eaten in three days. Many had gone the short distance to Fort Miamis to get food. Only half their forces were present when Wayne attacked with 2,200 regulars and 1,500 Kentucky militiamen. Among those attacked was a young Shawnee named Tecumseh.

The two sides pounded each other. Wayne's mounted militia charged at the Native Americans and were met with gunfire and arrows from the Indians. The soldiers on horseback pretended to panic and retreat but it was all a ruse to get the Indian alliance out in the open. The confederacy chased after the soldiers only to be ambushed by Wayne's regulars. The Native American's counterattack failed in the face of cannons. Then Wayne's men advanced in a series of bayonet charges.

The Indian confederacy dissolved amid the fallen trees. The victors fought with bayonets and the other side countered with tomahawks. The Native Americans ran for safety to the British fort. It was there that they received the final blow when their British allies refused to assist in the battle or let them seek safety. Thirty-three American troops were killed in the battle and about 100 wounded. The Native Americans had twice that number.

Following the battle, Wayne returned to Greene Ville to begin a year's long negotiation with the defeated Native American confederacy. While those negotiations were beginning, the British and the U.S. reached a settlement on trade by signing the Jay Treaty (named after Chief Justice John Jay) on November 19, 1794. The British gave up six forts in the Great Lakes region and two on Lake Champlain. In exchange, the U.S. allowed the Native Americans access to trade with Britain along the northern border.

It caused a ruckus. Critics fiercely complained that it meant the Native Americans were still dealing with the British. The treaty managed to avert the threat of war and guaranteed increased trade with Great Britain, but tensions continued—culminating in the War of 1812.

Treaty of Greene Ville—1795

Gen. Anthony Wayne, Little Turtle, and the Native American delegates met on August 3, 1795 to conclude a document known as the Treaty of Greene Ville. Leaders of the Wyandot, Shawnee, Delaware, Ottawa, Ojibwa, Potawatomi, and Kickapoo tribes signed the treaty and agreed to move to the northwest portion of Ohio called the Great Black Swamp and to relinquish their other lands. Among the others present were Gen. Harrison, and explorers William Clark and Meriwether Lewis. Ironically, Lewis and Clark first met in Greene Ville. Both sides agreed to a termination of hostilities and an exchange of prisoners.

Though Little Turtle wanted cooperation with the U.S., Tecumseh was highly aggravated and stated Native American land was being given away. The boundary line ran from (now) Cleveland sixty miles south, then west to Fort Recovery, then south to slightly west of (now) Cincinnati. Indeed, by signing the treaty, the Native leaders had agreed to give away two-thirds of Ohio country—leaving only the Black Swamp area of northwestern Ohio to parts near the Cuyahoga River as belonging to the Native Americans. Among the Native leaders who signed the treaty were the Wyandot chiefs Tarhe and Leatherlips, Shawnee Chief Blue Jacket, and Miami Chief Little Turtle plus some Ottawa, Ojibwa, Potawatomi, Wea, and Kickapoo. Among the other Shawnee chiefs present were Red Pole, Pucksekaw, Black Wolf, Lame Hawk, Black Hoof, Keeahah, Captain Johnny, and Kekiapilathy. The treaty reasserted the Treaty of Fort Harmar from 1789.

Tecumseh was so incensed that he vowed to reform the confederacy at Prophetstown (now Lafayette, Indiana) over the next decade.

The Treaty of Greene Ville ended the Northwest Indian Wars (1785-1795) and called for peace. Now the U.S. felt free to claim most of Ohio and to allow settlers to move in, but the tribes were given permission to hunt on the land they no longer owned. The peace would not hold. Settlers began to enter Ohio country and the Native Americans were resentful. It would cause more bloodshed for the next twenty years.

Trouble on Scioto's Waters

Gen. Harrison at Prophetstown and the Battle of Tippecanoe—1811

In the aftermath of the Treaty of Greene Ville, Tecumseh and his brother The Prophet were determined to expel American settlers from Indian territory. Each one devised his own plan on how to proceed. Three years previously (1808) the brothers set up their community in Prophetstown near the Wabash and Tippecanoe rivers. The Prophet was a religious leader with a charismatic personality who drew large numbers of followers. He was constantly communicating with the spirit world and was prone to saying he personally received messages from the Master of Life. The Prophet's followers demanded his protection.

William Henry Harrison, also serving as governor of Indiana Territory, had pushed seven treaties with Native Americans from 1802–05 in which he exploited the impoverished Indians who were also prone to enjoy liquor provided by his troops. Later Harrison would be given the task of attacking the Native American stronghold of Prophetstown.

Tecumseh was miles away from the area trying to build a coalition to battle his American foes and stop their encroachment upon what he considered Indian land. He left his brother in charge with hopes that nothing would happen while he was away. The Prophet sensed that the American troops were coming to attack his village and encouraged his men to fight—declaring that the enemy's bullet would not harm them.

Harrison and his troops approached Prophetstown on November 6, 1811. The Prophet did not have the military skills of his brother and attacked first on the morning of November 7. Though Harrison's army suffered heavy losses, the Native Americans were defeated. The American troops burned Prophetstown to the ground and most of the disillusioned Native American confederation headed to their home villages.

The Battle of Tippecanoe was a significant defeat for Tecumseh. He set out to resurrect his coalition, but it was never the same.

Tecumseh Dies at the Battle of the Thames—1813

The Battle of the Thames, also known as the Battle of Moraviantown, was the last great battle against the British and Indian alliance led by Tecumseh versus the

American armed forces. It occurred on October 5, 1813 in Ontario, Canada during the War of 1812. The War started when conflict arose over British restrictions on U.S. trade with France combined with the American government's desire to expand its territory. Though many of the Ohio Indian tribes sided with the British, others sided with the U.S.

The American naval forces defeated British Brig. Gen. Henry Proctor in the Battle of Lake Erie in September, 1813, leaving western Upper Canada under American control. Up until that time, the British had command of Lake Erie. Master Commandant Oliver Hazard Perry's nine vessel fleet out-maneuvered the British and captured six British Royal naval vessels for a total victory. Proctor, stationed in Detroit, gathered his forces, and hustled east across the Ontario peninsula with 3,500 U.S. troops in heavy pursuit, 1,000 of which were cavalry and another 2,500 were soldiers delivered by Perry to Amherstburg. They advanced to Fort Amherstburg where Tecumseh and Chief Roundhead awaited to consult with Proctor.

The British and the Native American alliance retreated up the Thames on September 27. Proctor agreed to go as far as Moraviantown—a settlement of mostly Lenape Delaware Indians originally from the Gnadenhutten area of Ohio. Tecumseh and his warriors were anxious to begin a battle with Harrison's forces. They met near Chatham, Ontario but the Indians were overrun. They headed up the Thames to a spot a few miles east of (now) Thamesville.

The Indian alliance formed a line in a black ash swamp on the British right. Harrison ordered James Johnson to engage in a frontal attack with his cavalry. The British regulars and Proctor ran from the battlefield. Tecumseh and Wyandot Chief Roundhead stood and fought by firing their muskets, killing or wounding 15 Americans. Johnson was shot five times. During this battle Tecumseh and Roundhead were killed, most likely by Kentucky militiamen who were with Harrison. With their deaths, the Native American alliance disappeared, apparently taking Tecumseh's body with them.

The Treaty of Ghent, signed by both sides on December 24, 1814, ended the War of 1812 on the western frontier. James Madison was president at the time. However, there was still work that needed to be done through further negotiations. The British wanted the border to be the old Greene Ville Treaty line so that they could have a buffer between Canada and the U.S. with the Native Americans in control of most of the Northwest Territories. Harrison and Michigan Gov. Lewis Cass, of course, were opposed to that arrangement. Harrison and Cass met with the chiefs of many of the tribes in Ohio, Michigan, and Indiana. In the end, the tribes agreed to end the fighting with the U.S. and to assist in the fight against the British. In return, the U.S. promised to return to the boundaries with the tribes before the war. Those chiefs who signed the treaty included Tarhe of the Wyandots, Black Hoof of the Shawnee, and Capt. Anderson of the Delaware.

The treaty ended Great Britain's hope of reclaiming the territory it lost during the American Revolution. They withdrew totally from the American frontier.

Proctor was court-martialed and suspended for six months. He eventually returned to England.

Harrison was elected president of the United States in 1841 but served only one month before dying of pneumonia. Through his battles, treaties, and some claim, trickery, with the Native Americans he succeeded in snagging over 100 million acres of tribal land for the U.S. in Wisconsin, Illinois, Indiana, Michigan, and Ohio. Years before his death, however, Harrison would speak admirably of his old enemy Tecumseh, "If it were not for the vicinity of the U.S., he would be the founder of an empire that would rival in glory Mexico or Peru."

➤ Additional Information

Simon Girty is buried in Malden Township, Essex County, Ontario.

Gen. Harmar is buried in St. James of Kingsessing Churchyard in Philadelphia, Pennsylvania.

Gen. St. Clair is buried in Old St. Clair Cemetery, Greensburg in Westmoreland County, Pennsylvania.

The Fallen Timbers Battlefield Memorial Park and the Fort Miamis National Historical Site are in Maumee, Ohio. Both are designated National Historic Sites.

The William Henry Harrison House is located at 570 West Broad St. in Columbus, Ohio. It is one of only twelve brick houses built in Franklinton and one of the few original homes still standing. Gen. Harrison is said to have used the home in 1813 and 1814 as headquarters for the Northwest Army during the War of 1812. It is registered as a National Historic Place.

President William Henry Harrison's burial site and memorial is on the crest of Mount Nebo, State Rt. 128, North Bend, Hamilton County, Ohio.

Gen. Anthony Wayne is buried in the Old St. David's Cemetery, Wayne, Delaware County, Pennsylvania.

A historical marker dedicated to Capt. Michael Cresap is at the Logan Elm Memorial on State Rt. 361 at Wolfe Road in Pickaway County, Ohio. It states that Cresap was a Revolutionary War hero of Ohio, Virginia, and Maryland, whose military services assisted in gaining the "Dunmore Treaty" after the Battle of Point Pleasant in 1774. He died while serving in the Continental Army and is buried in Trinity Churchyard, New York City.

William Henry Powell's painting of Perry's Victory depicting Commodore Oliver Hazard Perry's victory over the British fleet in the Battle of Lake Erie is presently hanging in the rotunda of the Ohio Statehouse in Columbus. Perry sent the famous message to Gen. William Henry Harrison saying, "We have met the enemy, and they are ours."

The burial place of Tecumseh is unknown.

7

Blue Jacket

Blue Jacket, Shawnee war chief, was born around 1743 in Ross County near the Scioto River during a time when his tribe was returning to Ohio country in large numbers. It was an era when Ohio was considered prize land with plenty of rich natural resources and abundant game. Both the British and the French desired to control the same territory and suddenly Ohio country was a mix of three nations vying for superiority.

Among the principal battle chiefs of Blue Jacket's time were Cornstalk, Logan, and Red Hawk. Professional historians have argued whether Blue Jacket was an Anglo-American named Marmaduke van Swearingen captured by the Shawnee at a young age or whether he was born a Native American. Nevertheless, Blue Jacket became a talented warrior by the time he was a teenager.

It is estimated that the number of Shawnee in the Ohio country during the mid-to-late 1700s was 2,500 men. The skirmishes leading into the Revolutionary War began in 1765 and were fought mostly east of the Appalachians. Unfortunately, it had repercussions for the Ohio Indians. Shawnee, such as Blue Jacket, sided with the British who had been good trading partners. Shawnee were known as fierce warriors but also as intertribal diplomats. Their villages in the Miami Valley were used as an advantage to the British.

In 1768, the Iroquois Confederacy signed the first Treaty of Stanwix in (now) Rome, New York. It is there they relinquished claims to land south of the Ohio River to quiet the strains between Native Americans and Anglo-American settlers. But in April 1774 conflict erupted. Two Shawnee tribesmen and a Delaware were murdered.

A few weeks later eleven Seneca, including members of Chief Logan's family, were killed in what was known as the Yellow Creek Massacre.

Blue Jacket vowed to push the pesky Anglo-American squatters back across the Appalachians. The Shawnee and Seneca lurked along the shores and attacked those coming west by flatboat. It was there that Blue Jacket began to rise. A more cautious Cornstalk urged restraint.

The Royal Governor of Virginia, John Murray, Earl of Dunmore, was loyal to the King and was also personally interested in obtaining land. He devised a two-pronged attack on the Native Americans and asked the Virginia House of Burgesses to authorize him to recruit an army. He gathered his 1,700-man northern division at Fort Pitt and headed down the Ohio River. For some unknown reason, he veered west to the Pickaway Plains instead of continuing down the Ohio. When he came to Scippo Creek, Dunmore ordered a camp be set up and called it Camp Charlotte after the Queen of England. Meanwhile, Gen. Andrew Lewis with the southern division of 1,500 men, was ordered down the Kanawha to the Ohio River on his way to meet Dunmore. Col. Charles Lewis, younger brother of Andrew, fulfilled his orders to lead the vanguard out of Camp Union (now Lewisburg, West Virginia) with the Augusta County regiment. This would become known as Lord Dunmore's War.

Cornstalk's forces encountered Lewis's troops along the Ohio River on October 10, 1774 in the Battle of Point Pleasant (West Virginia). It was to be the last time joint British regulars and Virginia colonial militiamen engaged in battle. After fierce fighting in which Col. Lewis was killed, Cornstalk's followers retreated north, chased by Dunmore's men. When the Shawnee got to their villages on the Pickaway Plains, Dunmore offered to talk peace, even as another detachment of his militia was destroying Shawnee villages north of the Ohio River.

Hard feelings over several losses depressed the Seneca, Delawares, and Wyandots and they broke off from the Shawnee after the Battle of Point Pleasant. On October 10, 1774, a treaty was drawn up and the Colonial Army pulled back. Under this deal, British colonists would stay out of the Ohio country, but the army could settle in Shawnee hunting grounds south of the Ohio River in what is today West Virginia. Some of the Shawnee agreed, others did not.

In 1775, the Native Americans protested as Virginians added new forts along the Ohio River on Shawnee hunting grounds. By the late 1770s, Blue Jacket had moved

Trouble on Scioto's Waters

from his village along the Scioto and built a new one called Blue Jacket's Town at (now) Bellefontaine in Logan County. Other villages arose on the Mad River and along both the Great and Little Miami rivers.

At the third anniversary of the Point Pleasant battle on October 10, 1777, Cornstalk, his son Elinipscio, and Red Hawk traveled to Fort Randolph and declared that they would release their men from restraints of the treaty and allow them to go on raids. Capt. Matthew Arbuckle, Sr., who had built Fort Randolph, had the three chiefs arrested and murdered.

In 1778, Blue Jacket captured Daniel Boone and 27 of his men on the Licking River. By now the Shawnee and British were at war with the Americans.

There were invasions of Indian towns from 1779–1782, causing them to lose their crops and disrupt their hunting. By March, 1779, the five septs of the Shawnee tribe split over problems with the Anglo-Americans. Two-thirds of the Shawnee departed to Mississippi while others left to go to Missouri near Cape Girardeau where other Native American tribes were living. Blue Jacket stayed behind and was now second in command. During the next three years, Blue Jacket met with the teenage Tecumseh who engaged in fighting for the Shawnee.

At the Treaty of Paris (1783), which halted the fighting between the British and the U.S. Army, the British basically abandoned their Indian allies. They agreed to evacuate most of their western posts where they supplied the Native Americans. The British also ceded their rights to Ohio country.

Even after the Treaty of Paris and the British had ceded their lands, the skirmishes and raids between the Ohio Indians and the U.S. Army continued. The Shawnee were quarrelsome and stated they would not release their hostages. Eventually, some of the Shawnee signed the Treaty of Fort Finney (or the Treaty of the Mouth of the Great Miami) reaffirming the Ohio River as boundaries between Shawnee and the U.S. This treaty ceded almost all the Shawnee land

Eagle. The eagle is a totem for the Miami tribe.

in southwest Ohio. About one-third of the Shawnee tribal chiefs signed the treaty, the other Shawnee chiefs disavowed it. Violence between tribes and settlers would continue.

Two things occurred in 1787 that would change the course of Ohio history. One was the creation of the Northwest Territories and the other was the number of settlers who now hustled into Ohio country.

Gen. Arthur St. Clair was commissioned the first governor of the Northwest Territory and renegotiated the treaties. It was decided by authorities that the land would be obtained by purchase.

Many of the Shawnee moved north to the Maumee to be closer to Fort Detroit and their British allies. The British continued to purchase scalps from the Indians and would also sell goods such as gun powder to them.

Blue Jacket and Black Snake continued the battles. They were joined by members of the Seneca, Cherokee, Miami, Kickapoo, Ottawa, and Delaware tribes who had remained in Ohio.

By 1789, Blue Jacket had arisen to the highest profile of the Shawnee by being named principal chief of the Maykujay sept. He and Little Turtle, a Miami chief, continued their revenge against the Americans with a victory over Gen. Josiah Harmar (1790), who was commander of the U.S. Army in the Northwest Territory. President George Washington instructed Gen. Arthur St. Clair to pursue the Ohio Indians. It was followed the next year by a defeat of St. Clair on the headwaters of the Wabash River on November 4, 1791 where over 623 American troops were killed. It was the Indian confederacy's greatest victory.

Leading into 1794, there were several treaties that had been signed between the Native Americans and their enemies including the Treaty of Fort McIntosh (1785), Treaty of Fort Finney (1786), and Treaty of Fort Harmar (1789). Many of these treaties were signed after the victors plied the Native Americans with alcohol and offered sloppy translations of the English language. The confederacy of Indians was unhappy with these treaties and wanted to restore what they considered their country. They demanded the return of the Ohio boundaries to those of the 1768 Treaty of Stanwix. They agreed to meet the U.S. representatives for peace talks along the Sandusky River and asked that the British be allowed to interpret for them.

The Indians also wanted the U.S. military posts in the Ohio country to be destroyed, including the following forts: Washington (Cincinnati), Hamilton (Butler

County), St. Clair (Preble County), Jefferson (Darke County), Greene Ville (Darke County), and Recovery (Mercer County). Meanwhile, British Lieutenant Gen. John Simcoe had built Fort Miamis on the north bank of the Maumee River (now Waterville, Ohio).

On June 30, 1794, Blue Jacket's confederacy headed toward Fort Recovery to cut off supply lines south of Fort Greene Ville. Not long after, Gen. Anthony Wayne left Fort Greene Ville on July 28 with a large army on a mission to confront the Native Americans. On August 7 they reached the Auglaize River and eight days later came upon Blue Jacket and Black Snake's villages. Wayne destroyed them.

The Battle of Fallen Timbers, the last big battle for the Ohio Indian confederacy, would be fought on the Maumee River. It was to be Blue Jacket's last big battle too. Gen. Wayne sent word to the chiefs that he wanted to discuss peace. The chiefs gathered to talk at their own war council. As a result, they fasted and prepared for battle.

On August 20, Gen. Wayne's superior army attacked. Blue Jacket's forces, including Tecumseh, returned steady fire. It was not enough. The Indians barreled toward Fort Miamis and to the safety of their British allies. They begged British Gen. William Campbell to let them in but were rebuffed, deciding that war with the U.S. Army would have resulted. So much for the alliance between the Ohio Indians and their former British allies.

The dejected Indians retreated to Swan Creek (Toledo) along the northwest bank of the Maumee. They had lost almost everything.

Gen. Wayne wasted no time invading the Indian's territory at what was known as The Glaize, an old buffalo wallow on the Maumee River at the mouth of the Auglaize River. This was a hunting ground for the Ottawa and other tribes. Little Turtle's Miami warriors also had a town near there. Wayne's men built both Fort Defiance at The Glaize and Fort Wayne close to Miamitown as symbols of their superiority.

Representatives of twelve tribes, including over 1,100 members of the defeated Indian confederacy, gathered to sign the Treaty of Greene Ville to secure peace. The Wyandots (Hurons), Ojibwas, Ottawas, Shawnees, Weas, Kickapoos and others joined. The Ohio Cherokees and Seneca did not. The U.S. acknowledged that the land was held in common for all tribes—not one above the others.

The treaty was signed on August 3, 1795. The U.S. acquired two-thirds of what would become Ohio including the southern, eastern, and central sections—all land the Shawnee, Seneca, and Delaware had lived upon. In exchange for their signatures, the Native Americans received $20,000 in treaty goods and $1,000 per annum to each Shawnee, Delaware, Miami, Wyandot, Ottawa, Ojibwa, and Potawatomi.

In what is known as the Greene Ville Line, the Native Americans could hunt in the ceded area.

Blue Jacket retired as the Shawnee's senior war chief and moved to the American side of the Detroit River. The tribes wanted peace and agreed not to side in any war between the U.S. and Britain. Blue Jacket, even in retirement, came forward in 1805 to sign the Treaty of Fort Industry which ceded parts of northwest Ohio to the U.S. Blue Jacket did some traveling in his last two years and even gave an address to Ohio Gov. Thomas Kirker in Chillicothe. He died in 1808 at his home along the Detroit river.

 Additional Information

Blue Jacket is buried in Wayne County, Michigan.

8

Simon Girty

Demon, scoundrel, miscreant—these words and more were used to describe one of the most controversial frontiersmen of the 18th century, Simon Girty. Most American historians refer to Girty as a saboteur. He was a colonial Pennsylvanian who would become revered by the British, the Canadians, and many Native Americans, yet hated by his fellow countrymen. His career would take place during a time of turbulent changes as Ohio country was deemed an uninhabitable western wilderness populated by a few British and French trappers and a scattering of military personnel. Not so for Simon Girty and his four brothers. Their roles would influence Ohio's early history in many respects. Of all the frontier characters who took part in the various struggles for independence, Simon Girty was among the most notorious.

In the end, Girty would be scorned by Ohioans as a spy worthy of treason in the likes of Benedict Arnold. To this day, he is often referred to as "The Great Renegade."

Simon Girty, Jr. was born in 1741 in colonial Chambers Mills, Pennsylvania. His father was an Irish immigrant fur trader and his mother, Mary, was a British colonist. Around his ninth birthday, Girty's father was killed and his mother married John Turner, a militiaman. Tensions ran high during the French and Indian War and his family escaped for protection to Fort Granville on the Juniata River in western Pennsylvania.

In an unlucky set of circumstances, French soldiers along with a group of Indians captured the fort in 1755, taking Simon, his family, and several British colonists as prisoners. Simon's stepfather was killed, and his mother and infant half-brother, John, were given to the Shawnee. Legend has it that Mary and her baby were taken to a Shawnee village along the Scioto River. Meanwhile, older brother Thomas Girty escaped, but not Simon or his younger siblings James and George. James was given to the Shawnee and adopted into their tribe. The Delaware kept George while Simon was given to the Seneca who took him to a village on the south shore of Lake Erie.

It was there that fifteen-year-old Simon became a man. He learned the Seneca language, successfully ran the tribe's gauntlet, and was adopted by Chief Guyasuta. Girty wore a scalp lock on his head and dressed in Seneca clothing. His Seneca name was "Katepacomen."

Girty was a quick study. His talents as a frontiersman and interpreter made him an asset which both the British and Americans coveted. His skills at learning the various Native American languages became voluminous. He could speak more Native languages than any other known person and knew the culture of most of the tribes. Girty was also an excellent orator—a skill highly prized during those times due to the fact there was no written language among the tribes. His memory was so keen that he could hear a speech and instantly memorize it. No other Anglo-American knew as much Indian lore as he did.

Simon's adopted father, Guyasuta, took the French side against the British colonials during the French and Indian War. The French did not fare well—they lost their fort in Quebec to the British and then lost Montreal. Canada now belonged to the British. With the French defeated, the Native Americans realized the British were in control and they needed them as trading partners to buy gunpowder and supplies. To show the British they were serious about trading, the Indians turned in Mary Girty-Turner and others. In the fall of 1758, British Gen. Henry Bouquet seized Fort Duquesne and rebuilt it as Fort Pitt. The fort was solidly in their hands when Bouquet charged off to stem raids by Native Americans in the Ohio country. He used Fort Pitt to protect settlers moving into the region.

The French and Indian War ended in 1763 with the signing of the first Treaty of Paris. The Native Americans feared, with good reason, a flood of settlers would invade Ohio country. To stem the flow of settlers, Chief Pontiac roused the tribes in Ohio country to unite. In what is known as Pontiac's Rebellion, he headed a confederacy that included Ottawas, Ojibwas, Potawatomis, Miamis, Hurons, Delawares, Shawnees, Wyandots, and Seneca. Guyasuta and his Seneca tribe joined Pontiac to try and drive the settlers out. From 1763–66 they raided settlements in Ohio and western Pennsylvania and captured several small forts but could not take either Fort Detroit or Fort Pitt. A peace council was called. One of the conditions of peace was all Anglo-American prisoners were to be turned over to the British, including ones who had been adopted into tribes. Simon Girty was one of them. Girty reluctantly went to Fort Pitt where he learned both his mother and brother, Thomas, lived nearby. Brother James then appeared which left brother John as the only Girty whose whereabouts were unknown.

Shortly after this time the Shawnee brought in 40 more captives and among them was John. By now Fort Pitt was a thriving commercial center and businessmen needed frontiersmen such as the Girty brothers as interpreters and guides for fur traders. This led to Simon being selected to assist in negotiating delicate treaties for the colonial government. By the mid-1770s, the British changed the garrison's name temporarily to Fort Dunmore after Virginia's governor Lord Dunmore. Girty served as an interpreter and scout at Fort Dunmore for the British.

During this phase of his career, Girty became involved in Dunmore's War in 1774. Somewhere in his travels through Virginia he met frontiersman Simon Kenton and they became close friends. He would also meet Col. William Crawford who later would meet a horrible death in northwest Ohio by the hands of the Delaware and Wyandots. Girty was promised an officer's position in the regular army but did not get it. His raw personality and irascible temper most likely caused the British military to change their minds.

Leading into the American's declaring their independence from the Crown, both British and American rebels wanted the Native Americans on their side. It was a confusing time for the tribes. Most of them liked the British but wondered what would happen to them if the American rebels prevailed. They would ask the question in their councils, "Would we be better off?"

During this time, all but the Mohawks of the Six Nations wanted neutrality and sided with the British. Girty was sent on a diplomatic mission with American Capt. James Woods to the Native Americans to invite them to a conference in Pittsburgh. Girty and Woods promised the chiefs they could keep their land if they remained neutral. The Delaware were receptive but not the Seneca or Shawnee. Later in the year Guyasuta spoke at a meeting with commissioners from the Continental Congress at Pittsburgh. Girty served as interpreter for his old mentor. Again, the Native Americans were promised the Ohio River would be a boundary between Anglo-Americans and Native lands.

Girty was sent by another commissioner to prevent trouble between the Indians and people of Pittsburgh. The city on the Monongahela had a combination of frontiersmen, keel boat captains, fur traders, and British loyalists. Pittsburgh was positioned in a strategic location with overland trails and several rivers—one leading to the heavily trafficked Ohio River.

On July 4, 1776, Girty declared he would fight with the Americans for independence. The rebels believed they would not have to worry about the Indians being involved. However, the key to neutrality sat with the pledge that the Ohio River would be a permanent boundary.

Girty's temperament and obstinacy soon soured the American military officers against him as he had the British. He drank too much at times and fought with other men. In 1777, he was arrested for treason when someone reported he had sided with the British to plan the seizure of Fort Pitt. Eventually he was acquitted, but he secretly seethed at the episode.

American Gen. Edward Hand hired Girty as an interpreter and scout to assist him at Pittsburgh. He sent Girty to the Senecas to inquire if they were siding with the British, hoping they were not. On November 14, 1777, Girty visited his old friends and received a surprise. He expected to be greeted fondly by Guyasuta, but his former mentor turned angry and called Girty a traitor. The chief felt Americans sought to cheat his tribe.

Girty reported back that the Senecas intended war. Gen. Hand wanted to strike the British and their Native American allies at their post 100 miles from Pittsburgh. Hand needed men so he sought the help of Col. Crawford, a colleague of Gen. George Washington. Crawford knew Girty and agreed to help. On February 8, 1778, Hand and Crawford led a group of 500 ill-prepared militiamen out of Pittsburgh. The officers did not seek Girty's advice on the best route. They stumbled into bad weather and turned back but not before a group broke off along the Beaver River and killed peaceful Delaware chief Capt. Pipe's mother and brother, along with others, in what became known as the Squaw Campaign.

It was here that Girty had an epiphany. He realized that if the British lost the war, the Americans would seize all the Native American lands even after their promises not to do so. Girty, Alexander McKee and Matthew Elliott slipped away from the Americans and ran undetected to side with the British. Girty was now solidly in step with the British as they dealt with Native Americans in the Ohio country. Once again, the Americans denounced him as a traitor and put a bounty on his head. That bounty would remain over him for the rest of his life. It would be a stain he could never erase.

The British did not exit from northwestern Ohio and the southern Michigan territories in the aftermath of the American Revolution. Fort Miamis (now city of Maumee), Fort Detroit on the western bank of the Detroit River, and Fort Malden across on the east bank were fully functioning British garrisons. The Native Americans knew that the British would supply them with necessities such as gun powder and lead. Simon and his brothers James and George were all hired as interpreters and guides.

When Girty, McKee, and Elliott turned against the Americans, they headed to the Delaware Indian village of Coshocton to seek their assistance for the British. The Delaware were so angry over the death of Capt. Pipe's relatives they voted to take up arms. Girty headed to Detroit to visit Henry Hamilton, the British military governor, to convince him he wanted to fight for the king. On the trail he was accosted by Wyandot Senecas who were skeptical of his claim of abandoning the Americans. He replied in the Seneca language that he was mistreated at Fort Pitt and was joining the British cause. When he finally reached Fort Detroit under the control of Canada, Gov. Hamilton hired both Simon and James Girty in his Indian Department.

Hamilton was hated by every American for buying scalps during the American Revolution. As a sad note in history, both the Americans and the Indians were known to scalp captives—a revolting act that gratefully disappeared after a time. In 1779, Hamilton was captured during a raid into Indiana territory and was taken in chains to Williamsburg, Virginia. Later he was released in a prisoner exchange.

One of the Girty brothers' first assignments was to join with Shawnee warriors on a raiding party in western Pennsylvania. On October 3, 1779 they spotted three American keel boats moving upstream on the Ohio River. They set up an ambush and pilfered gunpowder, bullets, rifles, rum, and silver coins. This kind of activity was going on constantly in the western frontier and along the Ohio River, causing great distress to the frontiersmen. Both Simon and James now had bounties on their heads.

Later in October, the two Girty brothers arrived in Wapatomica, a Shawnee town in the Ohio country. They heard an Anglo-American man was going to be burned at the fire stick. It turned out to be frontiersman Simon Kenton, an old friend of Girty's. Girty asked to address the elders and requested his old friend's life be spared. He pleaded that Kenton knew Gov. Hamilton and was an agent of the king. His pleading worked—the chiefs spared him.

Soon thereafter, Kenton was captured again by a few Shawnee seeking revenge for Kenton's attempt to retrieve some of his horses taken by the Indians. Girty defended him once again but the Shawnee were determined to burn him alive. They painted his face black as the mark of death. Fate, however, would interfere. The Indians placed brush around the fire stake, but rain soaked the area for two days and nothing happened. By the third day, representatives of Gov. Hamilton had arrived from Detroit and asked that Kenton's life be spared. They offered money and other goods in exchange for the prisoner's freedom. The chiefs agreed.

Though the British in Detroit looked upon Girty as one of the best agents in the Indian department, the Americans looked at him as a terrorist. Later his brothers James and George would also be called traitors. Many wanted to see the three at the end of a rope and set out to find them.

In 1781, Girty, his friend Alexander McKee and others aimed to outfox George Rogers Clark before he invaded the western territory. They rallied Native American tribes to join into a confederacy. Those joining were Mohawk Chief Joseph Brant, along with some Delaware, Wyandot, Shawnee, and Rangers from a British Loyalist company. Along the journey, Brant and Girty argued. Both had bad tempers and were known to drink to excess. Brant became intoxicated and struck Girty in the head with a sabre. The metal cut into his skull and put him into a coma. The next day Brant was remorseful, but the damage was permanent. Girty suffered periodic blurred vision and headaches the rest of his life. He wore a red bandana until his death to cover his damaged pate.

This was also the year British Gen. Charles Cornwallis surrendered to Gen. George Washington at Yorktown. The British may have surrendered in the East, but they were still active in the Ohio country.

The next year Girty would be present at one of the most egregious deaths ever witnessed. On June 4, 1782, Col. Crawford and Capt. David Williamson were leading 480 men across Ohio on a mission to fight Indians. Williamson was the officer responsible for the Gnadenhutten Massacre where ninety-eight peaceful Christian Indians were murdered. The Delaware had been actively hunting Williamson trying to seek revenge. Among the Indians were scouts Girty and Matthew Elliott. As the soldiers reached the Sandusky Plains, Wyandots and Delaware opened fire from a concealed hiding place. Crawford and the company's surgeon, Dr. John Knight, were captured and taken to Upper Sandusky.

Girty had known Crawford before the Revolutionary War. When he heard the Delaware had captured a "Big Captain" he went to see who was being held. Girty told the Delaware that the man was not Williamson, the officer responsible for Gnadenhutten. It fell on deaf ears. The Delaware were determined to burn him to death. Capt. Pipe stated that because Crawford was an officer of an invading army and wanted to kill Indians, he would die a painful death. Knight escaped and

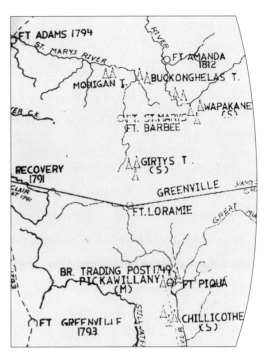

Girty's Town in northwestern Ohio is seen just south of St. Marys above the Greene Ville Line.

lived to tell of the horror. A hundred years later, President Theodore Roosevelt, an historian in his own right, said of the Gnadenhutten massacre that took place on March 8, 1782, "It is a stain on the frontier character that time cannot wash away."

Crawford was tortured for two hours while tied to a fire stake. As the agonizing hours dragged on, Crawford begged Girty to shoot him. Girty refused. By morning, as Girty left the village, the remains of his former friend laid in a smoldering heap. (See Chapter 9.)

Shortly thereafter, the British sent the Girty brothers, plus allies McKee and Elliott, into Kentucky to raid and discourage Americans from heading north into their territory. On their way south, their raiding party passed through a Chillicothe village where twelve-year-old Tecumseh lived. They made their way to a wooden fort called Bryan's Station (near now Lexington, Kentucky) but a strong resistance by the Kentucky militia held, with help from Daniel Boone, and the British-Indian confederacy lost the battle.

As the confederation of Girty brothers, fifty Rangers, and 300 Indians retreated, Kentucky militiamen pursued them. On August 19, 1782, the Kentuckians reached the Licking River near a salt lick known as Lower Blue Licks. As the Kentucky militia followed the trail, the enemy sprung a trap. The Rangers blasted their guns from the cover of trees, then the Indians took after them. They engaged in heavy hand-to-hand combat. Boone called for a retreat—his side was losing badly. Among the seventy-seven dead Kentucky militiamen was Boone's son Israel and his nephew Thomas. Girty lost only ten men. It is considered the last combination British-Native American victory of the American Revolution.

During the fall of that same year of 1782, George Girty, along with forty Butler's Rangers from Detroit, led an attack with 300 Wyandot, Shawnee, Seneca, and Delaware on Fort Henry in Wheeling. When seventy American soldiers arrived to help with the defense of the fort, Girty withdrew his forces. It is commonly known as the last battle of the Revolutionary War.

The American Revolution ended with victory for the Americans in the East, but life was anything but peaceful west of the Appalachians. Simon Girty still had a heavy bounty on his head. Unperturbed, his brother James and his wife established a trading post in Ohio country south of the Auglaize River which became Girty's Town (now St. Marys).

Though the main fighting was over, the British still refused to leave northwest Ohio. By now George Girty had joined his brothers in Detroit and was hired as an agent in the Indian Department.

Meanwhile Simon's reputation had spread far and wide. Among the words used by Americans to describe him were: traitor, turncoat, conspirator, and villain. His reputation grew so that his name was even brought before Congress in 1783 in disgust.

Ohio country was still a powder keg in 1785 and the signing of the Treaty of Fort Finney by some Shawnee on January 31, 1786 made it worse. Now that parts of Ohio had been ceded to the U.S., more settlers and squatters moved in and Native Americans grew increasingly irritated. It would turn out to be the fuse that ignited a bomb.

The Americans now considered all land north of the Ohio River and as far west as the Mississippi River to be theirs. On July 13, 1787, Congress acted to annex the territory they considered they had won. The defeated British provided land for the Mohawk tribe in Ontario along the Grand River. Nothing was provided by the new U.S. government for the Ohio tribes. Girty knew the Native Americans would still fight for their land. The big question was: would the British continue to help the tribes? The settlers were cutting down trees and driving away the game needed to survive. Hunting became difficult. Most of the tribes felt the land was their birthright and they would fight to keep it.

Another dilemma was the fact there were many American captives being held in remote Indian villages. Girty was given the task of finding them, guiding them to the path to Detroit where they could find their way home. For this, the Americans were grateful. However, his reputation for leading scalping parties and unending raids on settlements continued to sour his reputation.

A few years later Girty married Catherine Malott. He was forty-three, she was nineteen. Girty was given land in Ontario where he built a farm and hired men to work it. His neighbors were his old friends McKee and Elliott. Girty continued to work as an interpreter for the British in Detroit. He was a constant advocate for the Native Americans, helping them to resist American settlements in Ohio. The British liked the idea of an Indian confederacy because they saw it as a line of defense against an American invasion of Canada.

Girty assisted the Indians with their defeat of Gen. Arthur St. Clair in 1791 at the Battle of the Wabash. He was also present at the defeat of the Indians at the Battle of Fallen Timbers in 1794. His last spy mission was at Fort Greene Ville in the aftermath of Fallen Timbers to check on Gen. Anthony Wayne. Subsequently, the British had to give up Detroit and other western posts in 1796 after Wayne's victory.

Girty retired to his farm on the east side of the Detroit River with his wife and three children. His last years were not happy ones. He drank too much, and his health deteriorated vastly. He was visited by old comrades on occasion, including several visits from Tecumseh. He did not participate in the War of 1812 because he was ill and nearly blind. He died on February 18, 1818 at the age of seventy-seven.

➡ Additional Information

An historical marker stands in the city of St. Marys, Auglaize County, stating "Girty Town—So named for the renegade Girtys, whose home it was." It was erected by the Ohio Revolutionary Memorial Commission in 1930.

Simon Girty is buried in Malden, Essex County, Ontario.

9
Col. William Crawford

In the annals of Ohio history, one would be hard pressed to find a more tragic figure than Col. William Crawford, a man whose horrific death is still being discussed more than 200 years after the fact.

Crawford was born in Berkeley County, Virginia (now West Virginia) in the Shenandoah Valley in 1732. In 1749, he met young George Washington who worked as a surveyor in Virginia for Lord Thomas Fairfax. Washington taught Crawford the art of surveying—a skill much needed at that time. They became good friends. In 1755, Crawford took a commission as an ensign in a rifle company for British Gen. Edward Braddock and fought with Washington in the French and Indian War (1752–63) as British America battled New France for domination of the Ohio River Valley. The French maintained only a few forts which were scattered throughout a wide range of wilderness territory. They had traded with the Native Americans for several decades and some had gained their trust. The French now depended on the Indians for support.

French-held Fort Duquesne sat at the junction of the Alleghany and Monongahela rivers called the Forks of the Ohio. On July 9, 1755, Braddock's army of British Americans was defeated, and he was killed. Washington was a close aide to the general and led the retreat to Virginia. Crawford was promoted to lieutenant.

Three years later, another attack was made by British forces on Fort Duquesne under Brig. Gen. John Forbes. Washington was now the commander-in-chief of the Virginia troops which became part of Forbes's army. Crawford received a captain's commission.

The army reached the fort on November 25, 1758. The two armies battled and the French evacuated, burning the fort as they left. It was rebuilt by the British forces as

Fort Pitt and became the staging area for an invasion of Canada. The Treaty of Paris was signed in 1763 which ended the war in North America. It gave Britain control of both Quebec and the Ohio River Valley.

Now in his thirties, Crawford headed to the Shenandoah Valley to farm and survey. He was appointed a justice of the peace near Connellsville, then, in 1773, he was appointed presiding judge in the first court in western Pennsylvania. But lingering under the peace was the fact that Britain could not pay for the expenses of the French and Indian War which led to massive discontent in the Colonies with the British Americans. Eventually it would become one of the reasons for the American Revolution.

At one point in his military career, Crawford had a young man under his command named Daniel Morgan serving as a wagoner. Morgan would become famous during the American Revolution for his unconventional battlefield tactics and rose to the level of major general. He led the Continental Army to victory in the Battle of Cowpens and helped to suppress the Whiskey Rebellion. In 1797 he was elected to Congress as a Federalist.

Another young soldier who became Crawford's acquaintance was William Augustine Washington, a cousin of George Washington. William Washington was a cavalry officer in the Continental Army during the American Revolution and was a commander of the light dragoons.

After the American Revolution, these soldiers were paid by the new federal government in land grants given to veterans of the Virginia militia in the Virginia Military District. Today, the land given to Gen. Morgan and Col. William Washington is downtown Grove City, Ohio. As was generally the custom at that time, the land was handed over to a broker who sold it to pioneers heading west to new settlements. Crawford's own half-brother, Hugh Stephenson, was also granted land due to his services in the army. In 1775, Stephenson had led the Berkeley County Rifle Company 600 miles from Virginia (now West Virginia) to Boston in twenty-four days to join Gen. Washington in an act now known as "The Bee Line March." In 1777, he was at Valley Forge and later at Cornwallis's surrender at Yorktown in 1781. He was given land to the west of the Scioto that is now basically the west side of Columbus.

Crawford and Washington remained friends after the French and Indian War as both returned to work as surveyors. Crawford surveyed the area along the Youghiogheny River (now Fayette County, Pennsylvania) and decided to purchase property in a large wilderness area. He built a home on the south side of the stream, known as "Stewart's Crossing," on land across from Connellsville that he farmed. On October 13, 1770, Washington visited Crawford in western Pennsylvania. Together they traveled to Pittsburgh, then a budding town of mostly fur traders and the looming presence of Fort Pitt. The two took a canoe and visited the land holdings given to them as officers of the French and Indian War, including some in the Ohio country along the Ohio River. The two could foresee this land becoming prime locations for new settlers once the conflict with the Native Americans had been mitigated. Both men were able to secure massive land holdings. Crawford even traveled up the Scioto River at one point and sensed it would be an excellent place to invest in land.

Crawford Returns to War

Crawford would not remain a gentleman farmer for long. In 1774, a conflict arose between the colony of Virginia and the Shawnee and Seneca nations. The Battle of Point Pleasant along the Ohio River occurred on October 10, 1774. Hand-to-hand combat continued for several hours. In the end, seventy-five Virginia militiamen were killed and an estimated similar number of Native Americans. The battle culminated with Lord Dunmore meeting with the Indians at Camp Charlotte in a Shawnee village along the Scioto River in the Pickaway Plains (now Circleville area) where his main army was garrisoned. At that meeting, the Native Americans, including Cornstalk, rescinded their right to hunt beyond the Ohio River in western Pennsylvania, West Virginia, and Kentucky. Cornstalk promised to seek peace. Crawford, who had been called back into military service, was stationed at Camp Charlotte but had not been in the Battle at Point Pleasant. He was, however, present in the camp while the treaty was being signed nine days later.

The treaty ended what is known as Lord Dunmore's War, but it did not end the fighting. Dunmore sent Crawford and 240 men north to destroy Seneca/Mingo villages. Crawford knew the main waterways. The Seneca loved the rich bottom land near the Scioto River and had three camps located in (now) Columbus. They were known as Salt Lick Town or Mingo Town. One of them was located along the east side of the Scioto River where the Arena District sits today. Another was located on the east of the Scioto River where today's Greenlawn Bridge is located. A third was possibly located along the west side of the Scioto where Broad St. meets the Scioto Bridge (today it is near the site of the National Veterans Memorial and Museum). Crawford and his troops destroyed at least one of those villages, killing five Native American men and capturing a dozen women and children.

Far from Ohio country, the bubbling kettle of resentment between Colonial America and their British masters boiled over at Lexington and Concord. Crawford immediately offered his services to his native Virginia and raised a regiment for defense of the colonies. He entered the American Revolutionary War service on January 12, 1776, as a lieutenant colonel and on October 11 was appointed colonel of the 7th Regiment of Virginia Battalions by Congress. He was once again serving with Washington.

In the fall of 1776, 600 Native Americans arrived at Fort Pitt to sign a treaty reaffirming the Ohio River as the boundary for Indian hunting lands. Among the chiefs present was Cornstalk who told the Americans to send Congress a statement that his confederacy lives by hunting and cannot subsist any other way. He also stated the Americans never asked for the Indians' consent to take their land. Nevertheless, they would stay neutral during the Americans' war with Britain.

Crawford's first campaign was the Battle of Long Island (September 27, 1776). He was with the future president on Christmas Day when they crossed the Delaware and fought at Trenton (December 26, 1776). The next week they fought at Princeton (January 3, 1777). Crawford also fought with Washington at the Battle of Brandywine (September 11, 1777) and Germantown (October 4, 1777).

Shortly after Germantown, Cornstalk and two other Shawnee returned to the site of the Battle of Point Pleasant where they met with Capt. Matthew Arbuckle, commander of Fort Randolph. Arbuckle had been a frontiersman who had once traveled the entire length of the Great Kanawha Valley in 1764—believed to be the first non-captured Anglo to do so. Cornstalk complained to him that settlers were violating his agreement with Dunmore at Camp Charlotte. Arbuckle, disturbed by these remarks, put the three Native Americans in custody. While confined, an angry mob broke in and murdered them as revenge for the death of an Anglo hunter in the area. War parties erupted along the Ohio River. In November, 1777, Washington had Crawford transferred to Gen. Edward Hand at Fort Pitt to assist with the fight against the Native Americans in Ohio country. Hand was also a colleague of Washington's as the two had served together in the disastrous Squaw Campaign.

There had been plenty of trouble between would-be settlers and militiamen versus the Native Americans in the Upper Sandusky area of Ohio country in what is now Wyandot County. These Sandusky Plains had long been a favorite hunting ground for Native Americans. Half King's Town and Capt. Pipe's Town were both located along the Sandusky River. This area was both the capital and a rallying point for the Wyandot and Delaware tribes allied with Britain before heading south on expeditions.

Gen. Washington's Western Department believed that security of the U.S. would be accomplished by carrying the war into Indian country. Crawford wanted to decimate the Native Americans who were getting guns and supplies from the British at Fort Detroit.

Many times, Crawford expressed fear to Washington about Native American war parties attacking Americans beyond the Appalachians. To make matters worse, most Indians had sided with the British who had been their trading partners. On May, 1778, Crawford was given command of a Virginia regiment under American Brig. Gen. Lachlan McIntosh who had succeeded Gen. Hand in command of the Western Department. Crawford showed he had the skill and courage to fight in the frontier. He built Fort Crawford in the spring of 1778 about sixteen miles above Fort Pitt and, at intervals, commanded the post.

In the fall of 1778, Crawford led an expedition under McIntosh against British Fort Detroit. They built Fort Laurens along the Muskingum River and Fort McIntosh at the confluence of the Ohio and Beaver rivers for two reasons: 1) as staging points for attacking the British, and 2) to fight the Indians. (Fort Laurens was the only military fort built in the Ohio country during the Revolutionary War. Eventually it was abandoned.)

During this time, Native Americans were bringing scalps and captives to Detroit in exchange for supplies. Crawford personally visited Congress in 1780 to explain the threat from Native Americans and urged a greater defense of the frontiers. He asked for funds to supply the volunteers and militia. Congress agreed with Crawford and answered by sending arms and material to Fort Pitt and other western posts for an aggressive defense of the frontier.

In the fall of 1781, settlers in the area around Gnadenhutten and the peaceful Delaware villages west of Fort Pitt were becoming apprehensive. War parties would pass through with captives on their way to Detroit and daily life was tense.

After the British were defeated at Yorktown and Lord Cornwallis surrendered on October 19, 1781, Crawford returned to western Pennsylvania hoping he could live in peace. That was not to be.

Trouble on Scioto's Waters

As Crawford headed home, the Wyandots convinced the Christian Delawares converted by Moravian missionaries living in Gnadenhutten to leave their village for "Captive Town" on the Sandusky River. The Wyandots suspected the Moravian missionaries David Zeisberger and John Heckewelder had committed treason by providing military intelligence to the Americans at Fort Pitt. They were ultimately acquitted but, still, the Delaware were forced to leave their harvest and go west to safety. Their supplies ran low and they were near starvation. In February, 1782, over 100 Delaware returned the ninety miles east to their Gnadenhutten villages to harvest crops left in the fields and to collect their stored food supply.

A month later the peaceful Delaware were met by a detachment of the Pennsylvania militia led by Lt. Col. David Williamson. Col. Crawford was not with them. At first, the Delaware thought the men had come to trade so they did not run. Then soldiers told the Indians they were taking them to Pittsburgh to feed them. The gullible Indians gave up their guns and hunting knives. Soon they were taken and locked into buildings. The militia debated whether to take the captives to Pittsburgh or kill them. Ultimately, the sentence was death. On March 8, militiamen murdered and scalped twenty-eight men, twenty-nine women, and thirty-nine children. Two children and several others escaped to tell the story of the massacre.

When word got back to Upper Sandusky, the Indians were enraged and immediately planned revenge. Americans in the East were shocked at the barbarous action when they heard the news. It was apparent to the new nation that Ohio country was a battleground.

After the Gnadenhutten Massacre, Simon Girty and some Wyandots set off on a spy mission. They ambushed two soldiers and learned Williamson's men had killed 96 Delaware. Girty returned to Sandusky and dictated a letter to British Commandant Arent Schuyler DePeyster in Detroit with a report on the tragedy.

Meanwhile, Crawford was asked to lead troops against the Sandusky Indians who had been burning homes and killing settlers. Crawford agreed. He made out his will with bequests to his wife, children, and grandchildren and left.

Crawford's Last Battle

In mid-May, Native American spies were coming to Detroit with information of increased military activity. DePeyster sent 100 of Butler's Rangers to Sandusky

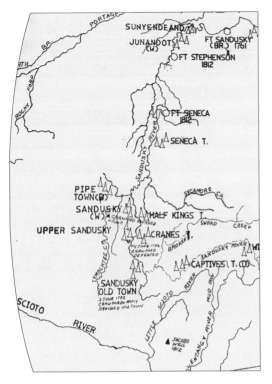

The Sandusky River showing Upper Sandusky, Pipe's Town, Crane's Town and Half King's Town where the Battle of Sandusky took place. Col. William Crawford and Dr. Knight were captured near Chief Wingenund's Town to the east of Captive's Town.

to assist. Girty was sent to rally the Native Americans. They assembled at Half King's Town.

Crawford knew the assignment to destroy Indian villages in the heart of Wyandot territory was a dangerous one. The distance between the starting points at Mingo Bottom (now Mingo Junction) on the Ohio River to Upper Sandusky was 150 miles. Crawford's forces gathered at Mingo Bottom and received a letter from Gen. Irvine commanding them to destroy the Native Americans in Sandusky. Many of these men had been at Gnadenhutten. The route would take them through the (now) following Ohio counties: Jefferson, Harrison, Tuscarawas, Holmes, Ashland, Richland, Crawford, and, finally, to Wyandot County. All but the last thirty miles was forest.

Crawford had four field majors—Williamson, Thomas Gaddis, John McClelland, and Joseph Brinton. Williamson was also second in command to Crawford. They vowed to avoid the Indian trails and marched through forests and swamps until the 480 men reached the last thirty miles of open prairie in the Sandusky Plains.

They left on May 25, 1782—with them were Crawford's son John, his son-in-law Major William Harrison, and nephew William Crawford. On June 1, they camped eight miles east of (now) Crestline in Crawford County. The next afternoon they reached the Sandusky River east of (now) Leesville. They had not yet spotted an Indian.

On June 4, Crawford's men reached Half King's Town on the Sandusky Plains near Upper Sandusky. They found the village empty but knew the Indians were hiding in the area. The men, especially Williamson, were anxious for a fight. Meanwhile, Capt. Pipe, tribal chief of the Delaware, lashed up with the Wyandots at an appointed spot and approached Crawford's men. A group of 200 Shawnee were also headed to

Trouble on Scioto's Waters

the area as well as an allied force of mounted Butler's Rangers from Detroit sent by DePeyster. Simon Girty was there as a British scout. Girty had known Crawford years before when he sided with the Americans.

At noon, the men stopped for lunch and Crawford sent his scouts ahead to look for the enemy. Not far along the trail, the Native Americans opened fire on them. The Battle of Sandusky had begun.

Crawford rode in with reinforcements and ordered they take a defensive position behind a grove of trees. By now others in the Indian confederacy, including British Rangers, were hustling to the site with Capt. Pipe in command. For the next few hours both sides shot at each other. When the firing finally ceased, each side suffered at least five deaths.

Overnight an unknown number of Crawford's men deserted. Meanwhile, the Native Americans gained more reinforcements, including 140 Shawnee and several dozen "Lake Indians." They had the area surrounded.

The shooting began at dawn the next day. What Crawford's rivals lacked in numbers, they overwhelmingly made up in zeal. Crawford still had about 300 men fighting the enemy. By afternoon, the Native Americans were reinforced by Butler's Rangers coming from the north. Another 200 Shawnee were spotted coming from the south. The enemy was now on both sides of Crawford's soldiers. It was at this point that Crawford made a command decision. His supplies were running out. The weather had been extremely hot, and they were almost out of fresh water. They were outnumbered on two sides by the Indians. Crawford declared a retreat.

Crawford's plan was to head his four divisions south at nightfall. Preparations were made to place the severely wounded men on biers and take them home. The dead were buried and fires lit above the graves to disguise them.

The divisions were to leave in two columns in case they had to fight the alerted enemy. One division led by Major McClelland left first. It was getting dark as they headed out. As the men broke from the woods, the Indians shot at them in the dark, causing panic. McClelland fell from his horse and was captured. Capt. John Hardin and his militia left prematurely and rode north from the woods, possibly to turn east and escape across the Sandusky River. Crawford heard of this and headed out to stop them. Sentinels spotted the men and fired. Another division of Crawford's troops headed south. Now a second band of Native Americans knew the enemy was near. Soon the frenzied Delaware and Shawnee were closing in. Panic caused some of

Crawford's men to ride unknowingly into a marsh—bogging down their horses in the muck. They dismounted and fled on foot with the Native Americans in heavy pursuit.

Mass confusion swirled in an aura of yelps, screams, and disorder. Crawford became separated from his son, son-in-law, and nephew and went searching for them among the turmoil. In the confusion, Crawford and Dr. Knight were left behind.

Williamson and at least forty men broke off and escaped. In their wake, at least fifty Americans were dead before sunrise—many of them tomahawked. Among the dead was McClelland.

The bulk of Crawford's men rode through the night finally stopping at a deserted Wyandot village called Old Town. They discovered Crawford was missing, along with Knight and scout John Slover. In Crawford's absence, Williamson took command. Also missing were Major Harrison and William Crawford, the colonel's nephew.

The retreating army headed toward the eastern edge of the Plains (now Whetstone Township, Crawford County) not far from a branch of the Olentangy River. A storm was brewing. Suddenly the Native American confederacy appeared on horseback at the troop's front, left, and rear flanks. A scrimmage known as The Battle of Olentangy had begun.

The two sides fired at each other for about an hour until a downpour drenched the area. Firearms did not function and the Indians fell back. Crawford's troops resumed their retreat. They camped nearby for the night unsure whether the new day would bring more fighting. They resumed their retreat without incident, returning to Fort Pitt on June 14.

Separated from his men as he searched for his relatives, Crawford and Dr. Knight were captured by the Indians along the Sandusky River not far from Chief Wingenund's camp in what is now Wyandot County. They were beaten and taken to a Delaware village on the east bank of the Tymochtee Creek where nine other prisoners had been taken. Crawford was still in his uniform as they reached their destination. The Delaware thought he was Williamson. The normally peaceful Delaware were now in a rage. They tomahawked the nine prisoners and conjured up a special kind of death for Crawford and Knight as revenge for Gnadenhutten.

Girty heard that a "Big Officer" had been captured who was destined for the fire stake. Often an officer was ransomed rather than killed, but the angry Delaware would not hear of it this time. Girty headed to the cabin where Crawford was being held. The humbled man he saw had been beaten several times. He recognized him as a former colleague—not Williamson but Crawford. The Delaware were still determined to torture him. Crawford asked Girty if he had heard the whereabouts of his son-in-law and nephew. Girty replied that both had been captured but would be ransomed. Unfortunately, both were killed instead.

On June 11, 1782, the Delaware headed out with Crawford to Half King's Town on their way to Pipe's Town. Dr. Knight had already been taken there. Word had spread among the Indian Confederacy that an American officer was going to be burned. As they arrived at Pipe's Town a crowd had gathered.

Capt. Pipe held a short trial. He told the crowd that Americans had killed friendly Delaware and Crawford was responsible for Gnadenhutten. Girty made one last plea to spare Crawford's life, as did fellow scout Matthew Elliott. Pipe demanded his tribesmen paint Crawford's face black (the mark of

A statue of Col. William Crawford stands in front of the Crawford County Courthouse in Bucyrus. Ohio is one of four states to name a county in his name.

death) and to proceed to burn him. The colonel asked that his life be spared but to no avail.

He was dragged outside the village to a spot along the Tymochtee Creek near a grove of white oak trees. His clothes were removed and his hands were tied behind him. Surrounding a fifteen-foot fire stick were thirty-forty men, sixty-seventy women and boys, plus one captured slave. The slave's main duty was to hold Simon Girty's horse. Dr. Knight was bound to a nearby stake and made to watch the ordeal. He was told he would be killed later.

Crawford's foot was tied to the fire stake, leaving three feet of slack. For two hours he was beaten with clubs. His ears were cut off and he was shot endlessly with powder which burned into his skin. The Delaware took sticks from the hot fire and poked him. He was tomahawked. At one point hot coals were thrown at his feet, so he had to step on them. At another point he was thrown upon the fire and scalped. In a last heinous act, Indians poured hot coals over his head while he was still alive.

Col. William Crawford

During the ordeal, Crawford cried out for Girty to shoot him. Girty refused, most likely knowing the Delaware would kill him too if he did so.

Dr. Knight witnessed the death knowing that his fate would be determined the next day. As the sun came up, Knight was escorted by one Indian guard to another village. As they passed the fire stake, Knight could see the remains of Crawford among the ashes. Somehow on the journey, Knight distracted the guard and escaped back to Fort Pitt where he met up with company scout John Slover, who had also escaped. Of the 480 men who had left for Sandusky, only 300 returned, including Col. Crawford's son John. Later, Knight and Slover would write detailed accounts of the sickening ordeal.

Upon hearing of Crawford's gruesome death, President George Washington wrote to Congress calling his good friend, "an officer of much care and prudence. He was brave, experienced, and active. So prominent a soldier and citizen had not, during the Revolution, met such a cruel death."

In 1898, over a century after the event, historians would write of Crawford's death in the *Ohio Archaeological and Historical Journal*, Vol. VI, "History does not record a parallel."

➤ Additional Information

An Ohio Historical Marker stands in Leistville, Pickaway County, near the spot of the treaty between Lord Dunmore and Chief Cornstalk in 1774. It was erected by the Daughters of the American Revolution.

In honor of the bravery of Col. William Crawford, counties in Ohio, Michigan, Indiana, and Pennsylvania are named after him.

The Battle of Sandusky took place in present day Crane Township, Wyandot County. The Battle of the Olentangy took place near Bucyrus in Crawford County.

A historical marker sits near the intersection of Long St. and Neil Ave. on U.S. Rt. 33 in Columbus that states that Col. Crawford and his militia had a fierce battle there with a village of Mingoes while the men were out hunting. Several women, children, and elderly were killed.

A memorial to Col. Crawford sits along the Tymochtee Creek in the Ritchey-Crawford Cemetery near Crawfordsville in Wyandot County.

A statue of Col. Crawford sits outside the entry to the Crawford County (Ohio) Courthouse.

10

Jonathan Alder

The Native Americans who lived in Ohio country had no written language, leaving much of their history to be passed along through oral stories. Fortunately, historians have the memoirs of Pleasant Valley (now Plain City, Ohio) pioneer Jonathan Alder for vivid accounts of his fourteen years living with the Native Americans.

Alder was born in New Jersey on September 17, 1773 and moved with his family to Wythe County, Virginia when he was seven. After the move, he and his elder brother David left their barn yard to chase down one of their horses that had strayed into a nearby forest. Both boys were captured by a band of Ohio Shawnee. David was killed but Jonathan was kidnapped by the group and dragged across Virginia and Ohio to a Seneca village in (now) Logan County. During the journey, Alder tried to escape and one of his captors grabbed him by his thick black hair and threatened to scalp him if he did not behave. The angry captor hesitated, realizing that the boy's hair, together with his feistiness, would make for a good Native American brother.

His capturers took young Alder on a long journey from southwest Virginia through (now) West Virginia to northwest Ohio through miles of dangerous mountain trails and thick forests. After they crossed the treacherous Ohio River, they traveled up the Scioto River to the Big Darby Creek in the Pickaway Plains. Eventually they reached their destination of a Seneca village along the Mad River that would become Alder's home for the next fourteen years.

After running the gauntlet, Alder was adopted by Seneca-Cayuga chief Succohanos and his wife Whinecheoh, a Shawnee. Alder had three adopted sisters—one of whom eventually married Shawnee chief Col. Lewis. Alder's new parents were thrilled

The confluence of the Big and Little Darby Creeks is in Battelle-Darby Creek Metro Park near Georgesville.

to have him. Their own son had died, and they longed to have another one. They treated him with great kindness and taught him both the Seneca and Shawnee customs and languages. At first, he had trouble adjusting to his new life. He was homesick and he had to adjust to the food, but young Alder soon began to enjoy his new life.

Growing into his teens, Alder hunted and traded alongside his adoptive tribe. Alder was well liked by his peers and could run and play games as well as anyone. He learned to fight and he also learned to love—eventually marrying a Native American woman but later divorcing her.

The men of the tribe were hunters and Alder was well taught. He became an excellent shot. As he matured, he helped to feed his fellow Seneca with game and helped clothe them with hides.

Violent conflicts between Europeans and Native Americans raged intermittently throughout the Ohio Valley from the 1750s until the end of the Revolutionary War in 1782. Two years after Alder was captured, the Treaty of Paris declared the land north and west of the Ohio River as belonging to the U.S. The Americans declared themselves victors and claimed Ohio country as their own. Most Native Americans living in Ohio country aligned themselves with the British, including Alder's adopted father. They disowned the treaty, declaring they would continue to fight against American expansion. They could get ammo and supplies in British-controlled Detroit. Alder would follow their lead.

The Native American chiefs Blue Jacket, Little Turtle, and others defeated two American expeditions in 1790–91, one of which was against Gen. Arthur St. Clair. St. Clair left Fort Washington (now Cincinnati) in September 1791 and led an army of mostly untrained militiamen north until he came to the Wabash River near some Miami villages. Here Little Turtle attacked on November 4, 1791. Many of the militia ran off. Another 623 soldiers were killed, and hundreds wounded. Little Turtle and his men had completed their greatest victory.

In June 1794, Jonathan Alder was along as Blue Jacket, Little Turtle, and American turncoat Simon Girty led an attack on a pack train at Fort Recovery with a large band of Shawnee, Miami, Delaware, and Ottawa.

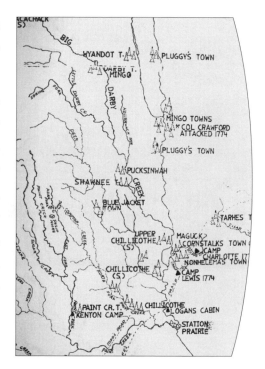

 Map of the Scioto River showing Chillicothe, Nonhelema's Town, Cornstalk's Town, Camp Charlotte, Maguck, Pucksinwah (today Orient), and Mingo Town (confluence of Scioto and Olentangy rivers). The northernmost Pluggy's Town is today the city of Delaware. Blue Jacket's Town is today Williamsport. Eventually Blue Jacket moved to today's Bellefontaine.

The Native Americans captured 300 horses and killed fifteen of Gen. Anthony Wayne's soldiers. Soon thereafter the Indian confederacy attacked again and killed another twenty-two men, but the Americans held the fort.

Alder was among the Native Americans at the Battle of Fallen Timbers, but he did not engage in shooting. However, he did commit a brave act by assisting in rescuing a gravely wounded ally while under a barrage of bullets from the Americans. The Treaty of Greene Ville ended the conflict and some Indians began to leave Ohio country and head west.

Alder married a Native American woman named Barshaw in 1795 but soon ended his time with the Seneca. The couple then moved to the Darby Creek in Pleasant Valley. There were only about 5,000 settlers living in Ohio country in 1796 but within fifteen years there would be many more. Around that time Alder had to re-learn his native

The Jonathan Alder cabin in London, Ohio was built by Alder in 1806 one mile north of the present site along Rt. 142. Alder was the first settler in Madison County.

language because it had been fourteen years since he had spoken it. Once he rejoined the Americans, he began his life as the first pioneer settler in Madison County. Besides farming, Alder would serve as an interpreter for Americans communicating with the tribes. He felt peace had been restored and said, "I could now lie down without fear and rise up and shake hands with both (sides)."

Alder ended his marriage to Barshaw and in 1805 traveled to Virginia where he was able to find his birth mother and remaining siblings near the area where he was captured. Alder built several cabins along the Big Darby during his lifetime. He divorced his Native American wife and in 1806 married Mary Blount. They eventually had twelve children. In 1820, Union County was formed from parts of Franklin, Madison, Logan, and Delaware counties—hence the name "Union."

Alder learned the techniques of Native American fighting and decided to use his knowledge by joining Gen. Harrison's army during the War of 1812. He was elected a company captain of seventy men from the Plain City area. His company was sent to build a blockhouse north of Marysville along Mill Creek to protect the pioneers who had moved to the Darby settlements. The fort was the first one built in Union County.

Trouble on Scioto's Waters

After only a few weeks, Alder's sense of the enemy's position made him leery of staying so far from the American settlements and had the men return. Feeling his duty was over, he soon returned to farming.

In 1818, Alder was visited several times by frontiersman Simon Kenton. He also knew Simon Girty. In addition, Lucas Sullivant, founder of Franklinton (now Columbus), had many visits and business dealings with Alder. Franklinton was the first town settled in the Scioto Valley north of Chillicothe in 1797. Sullivant's village of crude cabins had about 200 people and many of those started trading with the Native Americans who trapped animals along the Scioto River. Gen. William Henry Harrison knew Sullivant and during the War of 1812 placed his headquarters (now the Harrison House) for the U.S. Army in Franklinton.

Gen. Harrison had recruits assemble in Franklinton and organized them into companies. These new troops had light training and were taught a few military movements before being sent to fight in hostile battles. Not everyone was obedient. One man was shot and killed for desertion.

On June 21, 1813, Harrison held the Council of Franklinton with fifty chiefs and principal men of the Shawnee, Wyandot, Delaware, and Seneca tribes imploring them to fight on his side. Although there is no record of his presence, Alder was undoubtedly there to interpret. The chiefs agreed to fight for the Americans. Chief Tarhe, Grand Sachem of the Wyandot Nation who once had a village north of Franklinton, was the first to shake Harrison's hand.

In 1897 a Centennial Celebration was held on September 15 in Columbus to commemorate the founding of Franklinton and its place in history. At that ceremony, Col. E.L. Taylor summarized the historic conflicts between American soldiers and settlers and Native Americans, "The cruel and vindictive acts of the Indians were largely the result of the cruel and vindictive acts of white men."

In the late 1830s, Alder dictated his life stories to one of his sons, recounting in colorful detail his years among the Ohio Indians. Alder's exceptional memory left an account of frontier life among the Native Americans that few people knew and is one of only a handful on record. His capturers had taken young Alder on a long journey from northern Virginia to northwest Ohio through miles of dangerous travel to the Ohio River. After the crossing, they then traveled up the Scioto River to the Big Darby Creek and on to a Seneca village where he would live for the next fourteen years. The route shows the importance of river travel during that time. It is a unique capsule of Ohio history.

Jonathan Alder lived during a time of tremendous change. He died in 1849 and is buried in Foster Cemetery located near West Jefferson just north of I-70.

> ### ➤ *Additional Information*
>
> Jonathan Alder's log home, which once sat a mile north of Foster Chapel at Lucas Road, was moved to London, Ohio, and is located at the Madison County Historical Society Museum on State Route 142.
>
> An Ohio Historical Marker stands at the entrance to Foster Chapel Cemetery where Alder is buried. It is located on NE Plain City-Georgesville Road (State Rt. 142) just south of Morgan Road.
>
> A memorial stone and bronze plaque sit in a small park on Columbus's Martin Ave. south of Broad St. near the spot where the Council of Franklinton took place. It was erected on June 21, 1904 by the Columbus Chapter of the Daughters of the American Revolution.
>
> Lucas Sullivant's Land Office of 1822 sits next to the Harrison House (built in 1807) at 570 W. Broad St. in Columbus. These two buildings are the last remaining original structures built by Sullivant when he founded Franklinton.

11
Tecumseh

Shooting Star

Tecumseh was born to greatness. Often referred to as "The Shooting Star," his introduction to life occurred in 1768 as a comet passed over the earth. Throughout his life and for generations after his death he has been called "Shooting Star" or "Crouching Panther." Tecumseh was a great orator and his tribe greatly respected those who could speak well before crowds of people. He had a swift mind and keen senses, making him unpredictable to the enemy. He was brave in battle, a true leader, and by the time of his death he would be known as the greatest of all.

The Shawnee were an Algonquian tribe who returned to Ohio somewhere around 1725. Their territory stretched from Ohio into what is now West Virginia and western Pennsylvania. The Shawnee lived in wigwams, dome-like structures made from animal skins, grass, or bark strips shaped over a frame of arched poles. His people had a rich and colorful culture.

Tecumseh was born in Ohio country, but historians have debated the exact location of his birth. Some say he was born along Massie's Creek near the Little Miami River in an Indian village known as Chillicothe (four other Ohio villages were also known by this name). This village served as the seat of the Chalahgawtha Shawnee sept. (Today it is the site of Old Town, three miles from Xenia. Presently the site is in an unincorporated community in Xenia Township.) Others disagree, stating his birthplace was somewhere along the Scioto River near present-day Chillicothe. His parents, Pucksinwah and Methoataske, had eight children, including a set of triplets.

Tecumseh was the fifth of eight siblings. When Pucksinwah was killed in the Battle of Point Pleasant, Tecumseh's mother was greatly distressed. About this time some Shawnee were growing restless and discouraged at the influx of Europeans stealing what they considered their land in Ohio country. Seeing other disheartened members of her tribe head for Missouri, she headed south—leaving young Tecumseh in the care of an older sister, Tecumpease. His youth was overseen by his brother Cheeseekau and by Chief Blackfish.

Year of Blood

King George III had proclaimed that settlements of land between the Alleghany Mountains and the Ohio River were prohibited as far back as 1763. He declared that land was to remain as tribal hunting grounds. Pesky squatters came anyway.

The year 1782 became known as the "Year of Blood" due to the number of Indians, soldiers, and civilians killed. In that year, Col. David Williamson and 100 men marched from Fort Pitt into eastern Ohio country where they attacked and killed ninety-six peaceful Delaware. The British learned of the tragedy and rushed to Gnadenhutten. The surviving Delaware were taken back to Upper Sandusky and then to a new village along the Thames River in Ontario. The Native Americans blamed Col. William Crawford for the massacre, even though he was not present, and killed him.

Years of bloodshed brought them to the culmination of horror in a lamentable vortex. Two years before the start of the Revolutionary War, Seneca Chief Logan was off hunting when Virginia frontiersmen led by Jacob and Daniel Greathouse brutally killed two dozen innocent men, women and children from Logan's village in what is known as the "Yellow Creek Massacre" on April 30, 1774. (The site on the upper Ohio River is in today's Hancock County, West Virginia.) Several of Logan's relatives were slaughtered and he was out for revenge. Years later, President Thomas Jefferson would call the killings "inhumane" and "indecent." Jacob and Daniel Greathouse were never arrested, but years later Daniel was caught and killed by Native Americans.

Meanwhile, the Royal Governor of Virginia, John Murray, Earl of Dunmore, wanted an "Indian war" to solidify Virginia's claims and headed up a colonial militia to attack the Shawnee living along the Scioto River. The plan was twofold. Lord Dunmore would lead his troops down the Ohio River from Fort Pitt (now Pittsburgh) while

Gen. Andrew Lewis led his men overland to the confluence of the Kanawha River and the Ohio River where the two forces would converge.

The Shawnee chiefs gathered under senior war chief Cornstalk to decide their course of action. They knew they would be outnumbered. Would they run or would they fight? To make the decision harder, Chief Logan was not with them.

On October 10, 1774, Chief Cornstalk's men attacked Gen. Andrew Lewis's troops at Point Pleasant. The battle raged all day and Tecumseh's father was killed. Once the battle began, tribal members became sitting ducks—there was no protection for them. About seventy-five of the militia were killed as were a similar number of Native Americans. Cornstalk wanted peace. Dunmore requested the Shawnee and Seneca leaders meet him on the Pickaway Plains about twenty miles from present-day Chillicothe. Interpreter Simon Girty was sent to find Chief Logan and bring him to the location known as Camp Charlotte. Girty knew Logan and found him on Congo Creek. After a heated discussion, Logan refused to attend Dunmore's meeting but agreed to peace. Cornstalk declared he would surrender all Anglo-American prisoners held by the various tribes and would stop harassing travelers on the Ohio River. Dunmore promised that no more settlers would cross north of the Ohio River. Unfortunately, the deal was only temporary, and the Native Americans were once again deceived.

American Revolution

The American Revolution was fought from 1775-1783 with few battles extending west of the Appalachians. On November 10, 1781, Cornwallis surrendered to Gen. Washington at Yorktown. Once the British lost the war and signed the Treaty of Paris, they gave up claims to land in the Northwest Territory, as well as all land east of the Mississippi River. They gave up Fort Niagara in Ontario and Fort Detroit on the west bank of the Detroit River. However, in 1794 they would go forth and build Fort Miamis on the Maumee River and in 1795 they would build both Fort Malden and Fort George in Ontario.

In addition, between the years 1778–1871, the Native Americans signed endless treaties with the U.S. government. In March 1779, the Shawnee Nation had a disagreement and split. Over 4,000 of them left for Cape Girardeau in the Missouri territory and the rest remained in Ohio. Most notable was the year 1785, when American

 Panther. *The panther is a totem of the Shawnee tribe. Tecumseh was often referred to as "Crouching Panther."*

officials at Fort McIntosh, Pennsylvania bullied the Wyandot, Delaware, Ottawa, and Ojibwa tribes into signing a treaty giving away land where the Shawnee lived in eastern and southern Ohio.

After the smoke of the Revolutionary War had cleared, American war veterans needed to be paid for their service and were given land grants as payment. The ink was hardly dry on the final signing of the Treaty of Paris when Virginia claimed (and Congress granted) a tract of land in Ohio country called the Virginia Military District. The borders included the Ohio River on the south, the Scioto River to the east, and the Little Miami to the west. These were all rivers traveled heavily by the Ohio Native Americans. (The southwest and northwest quadrants of Franklin County, Ohio are part of these lands.) Virginia proceeded to use this land to pay their veterans. The fact these 4.2 million acres belonged to the Native Americans at the time was totally ignored.

The first permanent settlement in this land was Massie's Station named after explorer Nathaniel Massie in 1790. The site was previously used by Native Americans to attack settlers traveling along the Ohio River. As an interesting note in history, the land left unclaimed by veterans was given to the state of Ohio. In 1872, the Ohio Legislature used the income from this land to create an endowment for The Ohio State University.

Suddenly an influx of settlers crossed the Appalachians and began to put down roots in what is now Ohio, Kentucky, and Tennessee.

Raids

Now in his mid-teens, Tecumseh began to lead raids across Kentucky and Tennessee. He was a skilled hunter by now and an excellent addition to the tribe. Elderly

Chief Moluntha signed the Treaty of Fort Finney, also known as the Treaty at the Mouth of the Miami, on January 31, 1786. Shawnee leaders agreed to give up claims to their land in the southwestern Ohio country and in the southern Indiana territory. The Americans, once again, promised to keep squatters from land reserved for Native Americans. Unfortunately for the Shawnee, the new American citizens in Kentucky decided to form a militia under frontiersman Benjamin Logan.

In October of 1786, a Kentucky militia under Gen. Benjamin Logan, burned thirteen Shawnee villages along the Little Miami River and the Mad River of mostly defenseless women and children. The villages were left vulnerable when the men in these dwellings left to defend Chief Little Turtle from the forces up the Wabash River against George Rogers Clark. Chief Moluntha surrendered in the raid but was murdered anyway. In turn, the Shawnee formed war parties to harass Logan.

Warrior

The lure of the West and open lands enticed another 600 Shawnee and Delaware families to leave Ohio country. The tall, physically strong Tecumseh traveled along with them—his reputation as a courageous warrior growing. The group was discouraged that the days when buffalo were plentiful in places such as the Pickaway and Darby plains were now disappearing. Tecumseh was looking at other areas to roam and when the Shawnee and Delaware groups passed through Tennessee, Tecumseh decided to remain there for two years.

In September of 1791, the chiefs assembled at the mouth of the Auglaize River and selected the Miami's Chief Little Turtle as their principal warrior with Shawnee Blue Jacket second in command. The Wyandot's Chief Tarhe (Crane) was third. A few months later, Gen. Arthur St. Clair led his army out of Fort Washington (Cincinnati) with 1,400 men. He ordered the construction of Fort Hamilton farther north then ordered Fort Jefferson be constructed beyond that. Little did he know that Tecumseh was spying on him. By now the weather had turned bitter cold and St. Clair discovered thousands of Native Americans under Little Turtle and Blue Jacket were waiting to ambush him. They retreated to Fort Washington.

By 1792, Tecumseh was back in the area that is now Defiance, Ohio at the junction of the Maumee and Auglaize rivers. The Shawnee chief put out the call for an intertribal conference which drew Native Americans from as far northeast as the St. Lawrence River and as far south as Alabama. Both Tecumseh and Blue Jacket attended. The groundwork was being laid for a confederation to fight against the growing threat of American settlers invading their life. Tecumseh sought a great military and political alliance and eventually would travel from Canada to the deep South to try and establish it.

Indian scouts combing western Ohio spotted Major General Anthony Wayne building a series of forts to secure his supply and communications lines.

In June of 1794, Tecumseh and Blue Jacket had amassed their own army of 1,200 warriors. Their first attack was Fort Recovery where U.S. Captain Alexander Gibson's troops fought off the Indians. Again, the twenty-six-year old Tecumseh was among them.

Fallen Timbers

The Battle of Fallen Timbers in northwestern Ohio was the first major victory for Gen. Anthony Wayne and the newly formed U.S. Army. The battle that took place on August 20, 1794 was led by Blue Jacket and Little Turtle. Many were killed, including Tecumseh's older brother Sauwaseeka, and it was a complete disaster for the Native American confederacy. When it became apparent that the Indians were losing, many fled to the formerly friendly Fort Miami, a British stronghold. The British turned them away. The confederacy was dejected.

In the aftermath of Fallen Timbers came the signing of the Treaty of Greene Ville. Shawnee chiefs Blue Jacket, Red Pole, and Black Hoof signed along with the chiefs of the Miami, Ottawa, Delaware, Chippewa, and others. Blue Jacket, who was in awe of Tecumseh's leadership skills, tried to get him to sign the treaty. He vehemently refused. A disheartened Tecumseh announced he was moving to a new village in an area he considered quite beautiful along the banks of Deer Creek a few miles from Darby Creek and seventeen miles west of the Scioto River. (Today this area is Deer Creek State Park, fifteen miles south of Columbus.) Several hundred joined him and made him chief. Second in command was his younger brother Lalawethika (also known as Tenskwatawa—The Open Door—and by spiritual name The Prophet), who was a medicine man. Blue Jacket traveled to Deer Creek to give him details of the treaty. Tecumseh swore he would defeat the Americans and gain his country back. Then in

October, 1796, his restlessness consumed him, and he declared he was leaving and moved to the headwater of the Great Miami River.

Family

Tecumseh married an older woman named Mamate and had a son. Some historians say she died, and some say she and the great warrior divorced but nonetheless Tecumseh put the boy in his sister's trusted hands and departed. Tecumseh was gone for long spells without seeing his son.

Both Lalawethika and Tecumseh were gaining noted reputations but for different reasons. The younger brother spent his adulthood drinking and rabble rousing. His reputation was tainted. As he got a little older, however, he developed a religious side. He had visions. His followers now called him The Prophet.

The Prophet was attracting crowds in Greene Ville to hear him speak and to learn more about his visions. He wanted a stronger reverence to the Great Spirit (Monetoo or Manitou). He railed against drunkenness, adultery, and intermarriage with Americans. He vowed to destroy witchcraft. He demanded the Indian confederacy follow Tecumseh's grand plan to unite the tribes against the enemy. Only by joining as one united Indian Nation could they take back their lands and live in peace. Not every chief agreed. Black Hoof, Little Turtle and Tarhe were three who valued their own tribal identities over the confederacy. When people opposed The Prophet, he became enraged and said they were full of evil spirits. When Gov. William Henry Harrison was told of The Prophet's actions, he demanded there be proof that Tecumseh's brother was a messenger of the Deity.

The Prophet ordered that all the Native Americans in Greene Ville gather. He then denounced the Americans and Harrison in particular. He predicted Monetoo would give him a sign so they would not have any doubts over his authority. He said darkness would come at noon in fifty days. The Prophet predicted a solar eclipse would occur where the earth would become dark as night and the stars would be visible. Indeed, the day of June 16, 1806 would see the sun high in the sky at noon and then disappear just as he had said it would. The eclipse blackened the earth for seven minutes and, with this darkness. The Prophet gained the respect throughout the Indian Nation that he so severely sought.

One thing Tecumseh and The Prophet always agreed on was their love for the Indiana territory. It stretched from Ohio country west to the Mississippi River. Within that range were very few American settlements—the Native Americans were almost totally free.

In 1808, Tecumseh and his brother founded a large village near the Tippecanoe River in the western Indiana territory at the confluence of the Tippecanoe and the Wabash rivers. They considered it a great hunting ground and called it Prophetstown. Here The Prophet demanded his people reject European ways. His town was to be a religious community.

This news soon reached Harrison who was in his eighth year as governor of the Northwest Territory. Part of Harrison's time was spent writing treaties with the Native Americans. His method of operation was to provide plenty of rum to the Native Americans to get them to cooperate and have them sign whatever he presented. The Treaty of Fort Wayne, alone, gave the Americans 2.5 million acres across Michigan, Ohio, Indiana, and Illinois. The Native Americans received two cents per acre, a ghastly deal. Tecumseh did not accept these terms and fiercely complained that it was not valid. Tecumseh then met with Harrison and told him so. He said that more than ever before he knew the Americans would not stop until they had purchased all the Native American lands. Altogether, Harrison would eventually wrestle millions of acres from the Native Americans.

Trouble Brewing

For all The Prophet's bluster, he had not united the tribes behind his brother's grand plan by the end of 1809. Without the support of the Delawares, Wyandots, Miamis, and Shawnees, they had no chance of becoming victorious. They feared the plan might disintegrate. The Prophet then railed that the confederacy should attack Vincennes so that the Great Spirit would destroy those who opposed him. Cooler heads prevailed.

The Wyandots were beginning to accept the idea of a united front. They vowed allegiance to Tecumseh and agreed to adopt the teachings of The Prophet. But something sinister was going on behind all this. Wyandot Chief Roundhead learned that kindly Chief Leatherlips was friendly with the Americans and had sold land east of

Trouble on Scioto's Waters

the Wabash to Harrison. Roundhead devised a political plot to kill the elderly chief. He arranged for a small group to vote on whether to execute Leatherlips for witchcraft and treason. The vote was yes. The old chief then prepared himself for death, which came in the form of a tomahawk to his head on June 1, 1810. (Leatherlips' grave can be found at the corner of Straford Ave. and Riverside Dr. near Dublin.) In the aftermath, the Miamis and Weas joined with the Wyandots into Tecumseh's confederation.

Tecumseh felt he had to do something more drastic to save his lands. He began traveling in 1805 by canoe and horseback to meet with other tribal leaders between the Mississippi River and the Appalachians. By 1810 he had formed what he called the Ohio Valley Confederacy—the largest band of Native American warriors in history to that point. Chiefs from the Ottawa, Ojibwe, Winnebago, Potawatomi, Kickapoo, and Shawnee agreed to join him in this endeavor. Some of the Wyandots joined but some did not. Shawnee chief Blue Jacket joined the confederacy but died shortly thereafter.

Land that was once exclusive to the Indians was now seeing a greater invasion of Americans. The new Northwest Territory was given the formal name "The Territory Northwest of the River Ohio" by the government. The territories that would become states were Ohio, Michigan, Wisconsin, Indiana, and Illinois with Ohio being the first. Tecumseh, however, took great exception. He claimed the land was the property of all the tribes and, therefore, his alliance needed to share in its defense and fight off the invaders. He wanted the Americans to vacate peacefully and head back to the original thirteen colonies.

Previously, Tecumseh sought out an old friendly nation to help him get the guns and ammunition he needed for the fight against the American Army. He headed to Canada's Amberstburg, Ontario where he met British Lieutenant Governor of Upper Canada Francis Gore. He agreed to send the requested supplies but no more assistance. Now Tecumseh was headed to the southwest territories of Alabama, Louisiana, and Missouri to recruit more warriors for his grand plan, leaving his brother in charge.

Meanwhile, Harrison gathered 1,000 soldiers and headed to Terre Haute. This would become the staging area for his planned attack on Prophetstown. He was determined to break up Tecumseh's confederacy.

Tecumseh told his brother not to inflict disturbances while he was away, but The Prophet did not listen. The Prophet's reputation had grown so that 3,000 warriors were camped in the area to listen to his speeches, getting them more and more riled up with each one. The Prophet railed against the Americans, calling them cheaters and worse. He predicted a second eclipse was coming and that it would mean war. On September 17, 1811, the eclipse took place and a series of battles, later known as Tecumseh's War, was soon to begin.

Tippecanoe

By September 26, 1811, Harrison had 900 men ready to attack. They marched out of Vincennes, the territorial capital, and headed to Prophetstown with Harrison as the spearhead. They made camp on the banks of the Wabash and ordered the erection of a fort, which they called Fort Harrison, and waited for supplies to arrive. Once resupplied, Harrison marched toward Prophetstown.

On November 5, 1811, he and his men were a few miles from Prophetstown where they camped and prepared for battle. The Indians got wind of the attack and crept toward Harrison's men, waiting to spring like panthers. The Prophet once again rallied his warriors and told them the American bullets would not harm them. A shot was fired and an Indian battle cry rang in the air. Harrison jumped on his horse and shouted directions to his men. The Prophet stood on a nearby hill chanting a war song and imploring his warriors to fight.

The Battle of Tippecanoe lasted for over two hours. As one Native American after another fell, The Prophet disappeared and so did his confederacy. The tribes scattered back to their homes, totally discouraged. The battle was a draw, but 50 Indians were dead, and The Prophet's reputation was in tatters. The Tippecanoe Indians, furious at The Prophet, declared him a false diviner.

Harrison's army proceeded to torch Prophetstown and destroy the tribes' food storehouse before heading back to Vincennes. About forty Native Americans remained to wait for Tecumseh's return.

A Shooting Star and an Earthquake

Tecumseh was unaware of what had happened in Prophetstown and was still on his journey recruiting warriors among the southeastern American tribes when he made a bold statement. He predicted a preliminary sign would be given to the tribes that a great star would flash across the heavens and would indicate that Tecumseh was still guided by the hand of Aashaa Monetoo, the Great Spirit. On November 6, 1811 that prediction would come in the form of a bright flash of light that occurred out of the southwest. The Native Americans interrupted this as a sign of Tecumseh's magnitude.

A day in the middle of December would turn Tecumseh into an even bigger legend. The earth began to shake from the Plains to the east coast. It began in the central Mississippi Valley with the center at New Madrid in the Missouri territory. It is estimated that between 6,000–10,000 earthquakes and after-shocks occurred between December 16, 1811 and March 12, 1812. Tecumseh was in Cape Girardeau, fifty miles north of the epicenter, when they started. As he was traveling back to Prophetstown in February, the earth was still shaking.

Tecumseh returned to Prophetstown in an ill mood, furious at finding the village in ruins and his confederacy torn apart. He knew he had to side with the British to get what he needed to fight off the Americans. But before he left on yet another long journey, he and his brother rebuilt Prophetstown and struggled through the long, hungry winter with the few remaining warriors.

Off to More Battles

Tecumseh left again for a grand council meeting at Fort Malden in Canada, stopping along the way to convince the Wyandot, Ottawa, and Ojibwe tribes living along the Detroit River to join him. His journey took four months. By the time he arrived at Fort Malden at the end of June, the War of 1812 had begun, and Tecumseh's Indian confederation was now aligned with the British. The British had recruited the various tribes in hopes that Canada would not be invaded by the Americans. They encouraged the Native Americans to build an Indian nation in Ohio just beyond the Canadian border to serve as a buffer against a U.S. invasion.

The U.S. army started the war with a series of defeats. First was Fort Mackinac, then Fort Detroit, then Fort Dearborn (Chicago). Their only victory during that time was Fort Wayne. Some historians say British Gen. Sir Issac Brock made Tecumseh a brigadier general. He once said of Tecumseh, "A more gallant warrior does not exist. He was the admiration of everyone who conversed with him." Unfortunately for Tecumseh, Brock, who was known as "The Hero of Upper Canada," was killed in

Tecumseh. A statue of Tecumseh stands on the grounds of the Springfield Museum of Art on the Mad River near the Wittenberg University campus.

October 13, 1812 at the Battle of Queenstown Heights in the Niagara area. During that battle, 925 Americans were captured. Proctor became Brock's successor.

Between January 18–23, 1813, the Americans were defeated at the Battle of River Raisin in Monroe, Michigan by British Gen. Henry Proctor. The British killed 397 American soldiers (mostly Kentuckians) and 547 were taken captive. In a heinous act of war, Proctor allowed some of the captives to be massacred by the Indians. Tecumseh was greatly opposed to such deeds.

Located at the mouth of the Maumee River, Fort Meigs was built to keep the British from advancing further into Ohio. It is named after the governor of Ohio, Return Jonathan Meigs, Jr., and built by the Americans in 1813 under orders of Harrison. The defensive check point was ten acres in size and included seven blockhouses, five artillery batteries, two storehouses, and about twenty artillery pieces. It withstood two strong sieges by the British and Tecumseh's confederacy and turned the tide for the American army.

The fort, not far from the site of the Battle of Fallen Timbers, had been attacked once by Gen. Proctor. British artillery carried on for five days, but the Americans held until 1,200 Kentucky militia arrived in early May, 1813. The combined British forces of 1,000 soldiers and the 1,200 Native Americans under Tecumseh and Roundhead were forced to withdraw but would return in two months.

Across from Fort Meigs lay the remains of the old British Fort Miami on the Maumee River—the site of Fallen Timbers. During the first battle at Fort Meigs, a detachment under American Col. William Dudley comprised of sixty of the 13th Kentucky Detached Regiment of Militia and forty-five U.S. Army troops were pursued by Tecumseh's warriors and led them into a forest. A Canadian militia stormed the

Trouble on Scioto's Waters

battery and killed several Kentuckians. Over 200 of Dudley's men, including Dudley, were killed. This became known as "Dudley's Massacre."

The prisoners from Dudley's command were hauled by the British to the ruins of Fort Miami and a few wayward warriors massacred twelve of them. Tecumseh soon arrived along with a British officer and made them stop. Tecumseh was furious that the prisoners had been killed. He was totally against that kind of action. Ultimately, the battle was a defeat for the British and the Indian confederacy. Among the casualties were fourteen British killed and forty-seven wounded and fourteen Indians killed and forty-seven wounded. Among those was Roundhead's brother Jean-Baptiste.

The second siege began in July of 1813. This time the British and Native Americans under Tecumseh tried a different tactic. They staged a mock battle complete with war cries and muskets blazing. Try as they might to get Americans flushed out of the fort and head into an ambush, they failed. A strong thunderstorm caused them to leave. It was the turning point in the western theatre of that war.

Vision of Death

After the second siege of Fort Meigs, the British and Tecumseh's confederacy marched to Fort Stephenson along the lower Sandusky River near Fremont in September, 1813. Fort Stephenson was of strategic importance to the American defense. Commander of the garrison, Major George Croghan, nephew of George Rogers Clark, devised a battle plan that would out-fox the enemy. Croghan took his six-pound cannon and a little ammunition and fired it from several different locations, making the British think they were being hit from additional artillery. The Americans held the fort and the British withdrew. Croghan was later presented with a Congressional gold medal for extraordinary bravery.

The British and the Native American confederacy fled to Canada with Harrison's army of 3,500 men pursuing Proctor and Tecumseh along the Thames River in western Ontario. Among the chiefs with Tecumseh was Roundhead of the Wyandots. Proctor arrived at the Delaware village called Moraviantown occupied by the surviving friends and relatives of those killed by Capt. David Williamson's troops in the Gnadenhutten Massacre in 1782. Tecumseh was anxious for a battle and confronted Proctor. He wanted to fight. Proctor agreed and they devised their battle plan.

Tecumseh dreamed that night that he was about to die. The next morning, October 5, 1813, he stripped off his uniform and dressed in the clothes of the frontier—buckskin leggings, frock shirt, and moccasins. Legend says he chose to go into battle that day with only one weapon—a war club.

During the heated battle, Tecumseh was shot and killed in a meadow, as was Roundhead. It was a decisive American victory for the Americans. Gen. Harrison once said he admired The Shooting Star for his abilities as a great leader and a great enemy. He even called him "an uncommon genius." Now Tecumseh was dead, along with hundreds of others. The Native American confederacy vanished. This was their last great battle.

Tecumseh's grave was never found. The Shawnee signed away the last of their lands in 1817.

➤ *Additional Information*

There is a statue of Tecumseh at 99-73 Thornton Ave., Cincinnati, Ohio, 45233 near Mariner's Landing and Mariner's Landing Marina along the Ohio/Kentucky border. It is also known as Sayler Park at Thornton Triangle, 7343 Gracely Dr., Cincinnati, Ohio, 45233.

The dying Tecumseh statue is in the Smithsonian Institute.

There are also statues of Tecumseh at the U.S. Naval Academy, another in Ontario, Canada, and one in the Shawnee National Forest in southern Illinois (Saline City).

Another statue of Tecumseh is in Springfield, Ohio, along the Mad River near the Wittenberg University campus at the Springfield Museum of Art.

An Ohio Historical Marker dedicated to Tecumseh stands near Greenville in Darke County erected by the Ohio Bicentennial Commission, the Treaty of Greene Ville Bicentennial Commission and the Ohio Historical Society. Another marker is in Old Town in Greene County erected by William Galloway, M.D.

The unincorporated village of Roundhead is in Roundhead Township in Hardin County, Ohio.

12
"A Wilderness Village Along the Darby"

(The following chapter was originally written by Grove City resident William Howison in the 1980s. Franklinton and Georgesville both had settlers in 1797 and are considered the first two permanent settlements in Central Ohio.)

Chief Cornstalk and Chieftainess Nonhelema

For travelers in the 18th century, the Darby Creek started at the Logan County wilderness post of British Indian Agent Alexander McKee of McKee's Station, and led through present day Union, Madison, and Franklin counties until its terminus in the Pickaway Plains. At this juncture, the creek emptied into the Scioto River near Kispoko, the village of Shawnee war chief Black Fish, just north of the villages of Cornstalk and his sister, Nonhelema, the Grenadier Squaw.

Along its course, the Darby passed through broad plains of tall prairie grass, tall enough to hide a man on horseback, to plunge into dark forests whose trees had stood since the glaciers only to re-emerge into the bright sunlight and lush grasses of the Pickaway Prairie. Here the beautiful Darby rushed to its destiny with the Scioto and flowed to the mighty Ohio River. Today the course is about the same, but the trees and grasses are gone.

The Wyandot, Shawnee, Seneca, and Delaware fished its waters and stalked the elusive deer in the dark forests and made their homes along its banks. Two villages were located near present state Route 665 in Franklin County and two more just south of the county line along the Big Darby Creek called Pucksinwah (now Orient) and Shawnee Town. (Note: both camps were considered by historians as small, transient villages.)

A memorial to Nonhelema, the Grenadier Squaw, stands in Logan Elm State Memorial Park near the site of her village south of Circleville.

Along the Darby's banks, the famous and infamous—Tecumseh, Blue Jacket, Cornstalk, Nonhelema, Jonathan Alder, and Col. James Smith—passed as they entered the Ohio history books.

By the mid-1700s, the Shawnee had several villages along the Ohio River near the mouth of the Scioto where British traders from Pennsylvania and Virginia bargained with the Native Americans. James Smith was the first Anglo known to live along the Darby Creek in the winter of 1758 with his Wyandot captors. A list dated November 15, 1764, showed the number of white captives still in the hands of the Delaware and Shawnee as follows: Newcomerstown—fifty; New Town—fifteen; Old Town—seven; Salt Lick Town—five; Bulls Head Town—one; and Grenadier Squaw's Town—six, a total of eighty-four.

Another list addressed to British Col. Henry Bouquet without date, but likely 1764, showed eighty-two white prisoners at the Lower Shawnee Town (Portsmouth).

Simon Girty and Alexander McKee canoed through the waters as they traveled from McKee's Station to the Shawnee towns along the Darby Creek and Scioto River to work their treachery among the Kispokotha, Thawagila, and Chillicothe Shawnee in the name of His Royal Majesty, King George III of England. Along the way they no doubt paused at the side-by-side villages of Chief Cornstalk and Chieftainess Nonhelema. There is no list of those who met death at the slow burning stake of Nonhelema's burning ground on Scippo Creek and other Shawnee towns in the Scioto Valley.

Though the Treaty of Camp Charlotte in 1774 prohibited the Native Americans from crossing south of the Ohio River (provided there would be no white settlements north and west of the Ohio River) this did not stop the squatters who rolled into Kentucky Territory and then across the Ohio.

Cornstalk and Nonhelema tried to hold the Shawnee Nation to the provisions of the treaty which John Murray, Lord Dunmore, signed on the Pickaway Plains at Camp

Charlotte in 1774 after the Battle of Point Pleasant. Using their tribal positions and personal persuasion, they held the Shawnee and lesser tribes in check. All that changed in 1777 in a brutal murder near Point Pleasant three years after the battle there.

The English kept supplying Cornstalk and his tribesmen with arms and ammunition and, in 1777, Cornstalk proceeded to Fort Randolph with his son Ellinipsico and Chief Red Hawk to warn Capt. Matthew Arbuckle of an impending uprising. They were arrested and days later killed by a company of men.

Following the death of Cornstalk, the Shawnee almost solidly sided with the British but Nonhelema wanted peace and remained loyal to the Americans. She lost her position and sadly ended her days as an outcast of her tribe. Following the split in the Shawnee Nation in 1779, the remaining Shawnee in the Ohio country followed a course of war with the Americans.

Development Along the Big and Little Darby

In 1790, Gen. Josiah Harmar received orders from Sec. of War Henry Knox to destroy Native Indian villages in the western part of Ohio. On October 20, 1790,

Darby Creek Historical Marker

A drawing of the Dyer Mill in Georgesville.

Harmar led 320 regular soldiers and 1,100 poorly trained militiamen into battle where they were defeated by Chief Little Turtle of the Miami and Blue Jacket, war chief of the Shawnee. These same two chiefs, along with Buckengahelas of the Delaware and Black Eagle of the Wyandot, and assisted by the renegades Simon Girty, Alexander McKee, and Matthew Elliot, destroyed the army of Gen. Arthur St. Clair on November 4, 1791. That battle took place where Fort Recovery now stands (in Mercer County).

Congress had accepted the Northwest Ordinance on July 13, 1787, establishing a government for the Northwest Territory. But it was not until "Mad" Anthony Wayne defeated the combined tribes at the Battle of Fallen Timbers on August 20, 1794, and the Treaty of Greene Ville was signed on August 3, 1795, that it was safe for settlement in the Scioto Valley. With that treaty, the Ohio Indians ceded 25,000 square miles of territory north of the Ohio River.

Migration into the Scioto Valley followed the river north from the Ohio, then along two creeks—Paint Creek in Ross and Fayette counties, and Darby Creek in Franklin County.

Trouble on Scioto's Waters

In 1797, two brothers, Thomas and Elijah Chenoweth, settled in the southern part of what is now Franklin County. That same year, Franklinton was established along the west side of the Scioto River. Meanwhile, on the east bank of the confluence of the Big and Little Darby creeks, known as Treacles Creek, a Mr. Spencer and his son-in-law Osborn settled.

Others soon followed: Messrs. Thomas Roberts, John Biggert, James Gardner, Samuel Dyer, Samuel Kerr, and John Turner.

In 1805, Samuel Dyer built his mill at the forks of the Big and Little Darby creeks, and it became the center of community life for the early pioneers. A man could get his grain ground and catch up on the latest news from the other settlements to the north.

By 1805, the Quakers had established a meeting house on the head water of the Darby Creek in Logan County and settlements pushed into Union and Delaware counties, still following the Scioto River and its creeks.

Settlers came from as far north as Claibourne Township in present Union County to use Mr. Dyer's Mill. A common sight along the Darby Creek was a settler with knotted sacks of grain across the back of his horse, and a rifle across his saddle. The more industrious, such as Andrew Noteman, brought his grain down the Darby by dugout canoe.

Village of Georgesville

In 1816, Thomas Roberts laid out his town of Georgesville along the Darby Creek on the hill near the present cemetery. The road between the old and new cemetery was the main road through town. The road descended Graveyard Hill and crossed at a riffle above Dyer Mill. At the foot of the hill was a log house. This was the stagecoach tavern stop. It was also the post office and included a bar. There were three large fireplaces where the tavern keeper would rake hot coals from the fire and cook a meal right on the hearth. The bar was a small closet which had a small barred window where the drinks were sold.

The first post office was called Pleasant. The name was later changed to Georgesville after the town was laid out. The first postmaster was Thomas Roberts who was appointed in 1815. The second was Thanas Reynolds who was appointed in September, 1828. The third was William Scotts, appointed in 1851.

A school was built where Lawrence Ferguson and E.N. Coberly taught. Most of the buildings were of log construction. However, there were a few frame dwellings. The little settlement of Old Georgesville consisted of about 100 souls.

In 1840, Abraham Wright settled in Old Georgesville with his family, which included son, George. Abraham operated a blacksmith shop, and many were the incidents related by him of Indian visits to his shop to have their rifles, axes, and knives repaired. It was difficult to obtain coal for the forge in those days, and, telling the Indians that he was out of coal, was surprised when they said they would supply the needed fuel, and even more so when they returned several hours later with it. This happened several times, but the source of the coal has always remained a mystery, as no coal deposits were ever discovered in the area to anyone's knowledge.

George Wright operated an old store and inn known as The Tavern. This was the last business place in Old Georgesville. He then operated a blacksmith shop for a time at Springhill, which is now present day Wrightsville. He later returned to New Georgesville on the west side of the Darby and operated a blacksmith shop there with his son, Robert.

An old newspaper clipping tells that the town was inhabited by several men named George and rumor had it that George Spencer, George Osborn, George Lambert, and George Sullivant named the town Georgesville.

The same article tells of the Wyandot Indians joining the settlers for church services every six weeks when the [circuit preacher] came from Chillicothe. The first known religious meeting was held in the home of Thomas Chenoweth about 1810. Rev. John Collins and James Quinn held meetings in the home of Elijah Chenoweth. It is said that the Wyandots would often attend Methodist services when the circuit riders would be there.

James Quinn once wrote, "In 1805, we entered the Scioto Valley and built a small log cabin. My appointment in the Hock-Hocking Circuit extended from south of Chillicothe to north of Franklinton. My pay was $100 per annum. I had 28-31 appointments to fill each month, and in order to get home once a month, I had to conduct two services a day. In 1805, a road in the Hock-Hocking Circuit consisted of an animal trail through a dense forest where the sun never penetrated and the streams back up each year until the spring floods would clear them, and a band of Indians was not an uncommon sight along these trails."

These meetings resulted in the forming of a class composed mainly of the following: Benjamin Foster and his wife, Thomas and Elijah Chenoweth and their wives, and several children.

Rev. James Hoge of the Presbyterian Church in Franklinton held meetings at the homes of John Biggert and Thomas Roberts. No church of this denomination was ever formed in Georgesville.

Ministers of the Methodist Episcopal Church preached at the homes of Charles Hunter, George Goodson, Simon Cochran, and James Walker and at the schoolhouse in Georgesville.

When the War of 1812 started with England, it was rumored that the local Indians would join with the British. Many families panicked and deserted their homes and fled south. At one time, a party of settlers fearlessly marched to the Indian villages far to the north "to ascertain if they had concluded to put on war paint and make the rumored attack." They found the Indians sitting in council, but no hostile intent.

The first settlers had been chiefly immigrants from Pennsylvania, Maryland, and Virginia, and in Madison County were found New Englanders mainly from Vermont. Shortly before 1840, a German element gained a foothold in the Darby Valley.

Other Developments Along the Darby Valley

In the year 1822, the Fourth Horseman of the Apocalypse rode his pale horse through the Darby Valley. To the north, a plague of squirrels ate a ten-mile wide path from the Darby to the Scioto. This same year, malaria hit for a distance on both sides of the Big and Little Darby Creeks in Madison and Union counties. This disease was said to be caused by the decomposition of the prairie grasses. At first, it had been the policy to set fire to the prairie each autumn, but as the area became more settled, this practice was discontinued for fear of setting fire to homes and crops.

During the few years that then elapsed, the prairie became a wet, thick mass of decay, and bred the germs of disease. Mosquitoes were such a pest, that deer would descend into the Darby after nightfall and remain there for hours with only the end of their noses above the water to escape them.

Further to the south, along Paint Creek, the year of cholera left many grieving for lost loved ones. Many were the incidents where a father, himself sick with the fever, had to build the coffin, dig the grave, and deposit his beloved wife or child beneath the clods of the valley. Meanwhile, in Fayette County, people had to hide the body of a loved one from the men manning the death wagon which came to haul the bodies to a common burning ground. Some were buried with little or no ceremony in the dark of night in remote family plots with no stone to mark the spot.

The Shilling house was the last building left in Old Georgesville and it was torn down years ago. The old road no longer descends Graveyard Hill. The grass now grows where once was heard anvil and the pounding hooves of the stagecoach horses as they descended the hill to stop at the stagecoach stop.

Atop the hill stands, like silent sentinels, the headstones of the Fergusons, the Biggerts, the Gardners, and the Kerrs, keeping watch over the little low land that was once a village in the wilderness.

> ## Additional Information

The author of this article, William Howison, was a long-time historian in the southwest Franklin County, Ohio region. Howison studied the Native Americans who lived in this area and documented artifacts from various tribes. He and his wife, Barbara, were founding members of the Southwest Franklin County Historical Society. Portions of a map he created of Ohio's Native American villages is included in this book. This chapter was edited by Janet Shailer from the original work with permission by Barbara Howison.

Monuments to Chief Cornstalk and his sister, Chieftainess Nonhelema, are in Logan Elm State Memorial Park, State Route 361, south of Circleville in the Pickaway Plains. In this park is also a monument to Chief Logan's Lament delivered under the famous Logan Elm tree.

A marker entitled "Cornstalk's Visit and The Negotiator's Escape" stands at the end of Lincoln Ave. between State Rt. 23 and the Olentangy River in Delaware, OH. It states that William Wilson and Joseph Nicholson left Fort Pitt to try and convince Ohio tribes not to join the British. They were accompanied by Cornstalk and other Ohio Indians.

An Ohio Historical Marker stands on a hill along Emerson Road 0.4 miles east of U.S. Rt. 23 in the Pickaway Plains marking both the site of Grenadier

Squaw's Village and Cornstalk's Town. Nonhelema's home was considered one of the primary Shawnee settlements in Ohio.

An Ohio Historical Marker is dedicated to "The Deercreek Frontier/Williamsport and Deercreek Twp." at the intersection of Mill St. & Main St. in Williamsport, OH. It states that in 1772–73, missionary David Jones visited the villages of Blue Jacket's Town and Pickaweeke. Also, Methodist Circuit Deacon Dr. Edward Tiffin met Virginia settlers here in 1798. Tiffin was elected the first Ohio governor.

An Ohio Historical Marker dedicated to Camp Charlotte stands in Leistville near State Rt. 56 a mile north of State Rt. 159 in Pickaway County.

An Ohio Historical Marker stands near the confluence of the Big and Little Darby Creeks at the canoe access at Alkire and Gardiner Roads in Battelle-Darby Metro Park.

Several markers are in Battelle-Darby Metro Park in the Georgesville area. They include: Ice Over Ohio and A Valley is Born (about glaciers), Back to the Same Old Grind (on Dyer Mill), and the Voss Mound—Site of the Fort Ancient culture.

An Ohio Historical Marker titled "Franklinton" is near the corner of Broad St. and Gift St. in the Franklinton area of Columbus. It is dedicated to founder Lucas Sullivant who founded the village on the west side of the Scioto River in 1797.

13
Exodus

The exodus of the Native Americans from Ohio country is a sad and agonizing story. Life on the frontier for Ohio tribes in the early 19th century was ever-changing and dissatisfying. The invasion of settlers into Ohio territory and the reserves set up for the Native Americans by the U.S. government through treaties was choking their way of life. Their attempt at learning to farm and breed livestock, though often successful, was unsettling and unfulfilling. They longed for freedom and a return to their preferred way of life. Their departure went as follows:

The Shawnee, Seneca, Delaware, and Miami

Even before the beginning of the American Revolution, life for Native Americans was changing. Some of the Shawnee and Delaware left Ohio and headed west to the Indiana territory and beyond to hunt and live their preferred nomadic lifestyle. After the Gnadenhutten Massacre most of the Delaware headed to Ontario, Canada where other tribesmen lived.

In 1784, with encouragement of the Spanish, a group of Shawnee and Delaware headed to the Apple Creek and Cape Girardeau areas of Missouri. Furthermore, in the aftermath of Washington's defeat of the British and the establishment of the U.S. Constitution in 1791, additional Shawnee tribes headed west. In 1803, some Shawnee went to Texas after the Louisiana Purchase. Still feeling unsettled, these same tribes moved to the Canadian River in Oklahoma territory.

There is no doubt that the Ohio and U.S. government officials wanted the Native Americans to leave Ohio. Territorial governor Lewis Cass, for one, wanted them gone so their valuable land could be sold to settlers. The population of non-Native Americans was growing and in every council house in every Indian village there were arguments about whether to leave Ohio.

By 1812, an estimated 1,200 Shawnee had moved beyond the Mississippi River. By 1813, Tecumseh was dead at the hands of the Americans at the Battle of Thames. By now there were only about 800 of his fellow Shawnee living in Ohio. So many settlers were pouring into Ohio that the year 1815 became known as "The Great Migration."

In 1817, the U.S. government and the Ohio Shawnee signed the Treaty of Fort Meigs (near the site of the Battle of Fallen Timbers) giving the Native Americans three reserves at Wapakoneta, Hog Creek, and Lewistown. These were shared with the Seneca, who eventually would become part of the Cayuga tribe. This, in effect, ceded all Shawnee lands to the U.S. government, leaving them with their backs to the wall.

James Monroe was president of the United States from 1817 to 1825. Monroe won the passage of the Civilization Fund of 1819 which made money available for schools to teach Native Americans farming and English. It also served as an incentive for tribes to leave Ohio for reserves in the West. Monroe's secretary of war, John C. Calhoun, was an ally willing to accommodate the Native Americans. Monroe did not see the tribes as a threat but believed they would be happier away from Ohio where they were crowded onto small reserves and basically living in poverty.

The Miami confederacy had been angry since the Treaty of Paris in 1783 ended the American Revolution and essentially transferred their land to a former enemy. The Miami were considered tremendous traders and fierce fighters and hated settlers heading north across the Ohio River. Led by the great war chief Little Turtle, the Miami dug in their heels and refused to discuss any treaties. By 1790, Little Turtle had become the supreme commander of the Miami confederacy. But in the aftermath of the Treaty of Greene Ville, Little Turtle knew things were changing. He died in 1812 but not before signing treaties from 1795–1809.

In 1818, the U.S. government forced the Miami confederacy to give up their last reserve in Ohio. Some headed to Indiana but eventually even those tribal members left for Kansas in the 1850s.

Monroe made a proposal to the U.S. Senate to move other tribes beyond the Mississippi and soon Shawnee Chief Colonel Lewis was sent to negotiate with the government in Washington, D.C. Territorial Gov. Lewis Cass declared he would come to Wapakoneta to negotiate treaties for the Shawnee to leave. Congress, however, opposed his plan. President John Quincy Adams, whose vice president was Calhoun, also failed to get approval from Congress.

Later Gov. Cass was sent to negotiate with individual Shawnee tribes to exchange their Ohio land for reserves across the Mississippi in May 1825. Cass implored them to leave—the handwriting was on the wall. They were surrounded by American settlers and life was hard, made worse by whiskey peddlers who hovered around all tribes. Cass told them life in Kansas would be like "the old days" of vast hunting of buffalo, bear, and panthers. Chief Black Hoof, now growing old, was unhappy and demanded his tribe stay. Other chiefs considered leaving. In the end, only Colonel Lewis left Ohio at that time with a mere forty Shawnee.

The next year, about 300–400 Shawnee loaded their wagons and headed west with Tecumseh's brother, The Prophet, and Tecumseh's son. By the time they reached Kaskaskia, Illinois, near the Mississippi River, they had lost one-fourth of their people either to death or dissertation. (Kaskaskia had been the capital of the Illinois territory until 1818.)

William Clark (of Lewis and Clark fame) offered a reserve along the Kansas River and the Shawnee headed there. Periodically they had to stop for various lengths of time to rest and recover. The Prophet was disgruntled. His disposition was reportedly so bad that his wife and nephew abandoned him. Trouble after trouble consumed the journey. The group did not actually reach their destination in Kansas until May 1828. The Prophet hated the Kansas territory. He died there, sick, and almost alone, in November, 1836.

Some thought the tribes should be removed for their own good and to preserve the peace. The Seneca numbered only about 550 in the late 1820s and complained to President Adams that they too wanted to move west. Settlers were squeezing them out of their main village of Green Springs. After several tries to plead their case, they found a willing partner in President Andrew Jackson who wanted the removal of all tribes in Ohio. Most of the Delaware and Miami had already left.

President Andrew Jackson was the seventh president of the U.S. from 1829–1837. For most of his first term, John C. Calhoun was his vice president. Jackson was a military hero who had barely lost the presidency to John Quincy Adams in 1824. He disliked Native Americans and displayed animosity toward them. In 1830, he implemented the Indian Removal Act which gave him power to make treaties that led to displacement of tribes from their homeland to territory west of the Mississippi. Jackson believed the land belonged to the people of the U.S., not the tribes, and displayed little sympathy and major prejudice towards them. This was quite apparent in his inaugural address in 1829 when he stated his intent to remove eastern tribes across the Mississippi. When the Indian Removal Act was voted on in the U.S. House of Representatives, twelve of the fourteen Ohio congressmen voted against it. Another one did not vote.

When word got back to Ohio concerning the vote, the remaining Shawnee were dumbfounded and so were other tribes who considered their land their birthright.

The Seneca were often called "Mingo" by both rival tribes and settlers, a term which was considered derogatory. In 1817, they had been given thousands of acres in reserves along the Sandusky River by the Treaty at the Foot of the Rapids. The next year they were given several thousand more at St. Marys. Just as the Miami, Shawnee, and other tribes were feeling hemmed in by the swarms of settlers coming into their territory, the Seneca chiefs wanted to trade their land on the reserves for new land across the Mississippi. They consulted with Indian agents to expedite their plan.

After the Indian Removal Act of 1830, with almost no game to hunt, the Sandusky Seneca signed a treaty with the U.S. government in 1831 granting them land in the northeast Oklahoma territory. The Seneca and the Lewistown Shawnee planned to leave together and head to Oklahoma. Meanwhile, the Hog Creek and Wapakoneta Shawnee planned to leave Ohio to go to Johnson County, Kansas.

It was an incredibly sad day for the Native Americans in September, 1832 when about 250 Shawnee and Seneca from Lewistown, about 400 Shawnee from Wapakoneta and Hog Creek, and about 100 Ottawa began the slow trek toward their new homes across the Mississippi. Reports from several newspapers of that time stated that a long wagon train appeared for miles along the Sandusky River. The tribe painfully and tearfully stopped at every Native American village along their route to say goodbye to friends. Their hearts asked them to leave but those same hearts were heavy at leaving the graves of forbears in their villages. The journey was going to be dangerous and the wagon train would only move about twelve miles per day on the 800-mile trip. Although some had doubts about leaving their home, they relied on the Great Spirit to guide and protect them.

Note: For more information on the Shawnee's departure from Ohio, the book *The Eastern Shawnee Tribe of Oklahoma—Resilience through Adversity* edited by Stephen Warren is an excellent resource. Another superb book is *Gathering Together—The Shawnee People through Diaspora and Nationhood, 1600–1870* by Sami Lakomaki.

The Ottawa and the Wyandot

The Ottawa first came to Ohio country in the 1720s—one of the earliest tribes to come into the northwestern part of the state. They were related to both the Potawatomi and the Chippewa. They had prospered in the Buckeye state but by the 1830s they were living on three reserves in Maumee River Valley. One was along the Maumee River granted to them at the Treaty at the Foot of the Rapids in 1817, another at Maumee Bay granted in Detroit in 1807, and a third one along the Maumee at Roche de Boeuf and Wolf Rapids.

They had a deep history in the state. Their greatest chief, Pontiac, had been born in the Maumee Valley. They had traded with the British and fought with them during the American Revolution. They had been defeated by Gen. Anthony Wayne at the Battle of Fallen Timbers and suffered greatly after Wayne ordered their villages, fields, and trading posts torched. Worse yet was the eventual defeat as part of Tecumseh's confederacy during the War of 1812.

By 1825, the Ohio and Erie Canal was completed, and a future canal (the Miami & Erie) was being planned to go from the Maumee Valley to the Ohio River. Settlers were cultivating the rich soil of the Black Swamp and many of the Ottawa had fallen into ill health or were addicted to alcohol. Their tribe was considered poor.

The Ottawa were told that land across the Mississippi had plenty of game and streams for fishing. Chief Ottokee, half-brother to Chief Wauseon, looked to trade their reserves for land in the west. Some of their chiefs headed a scouting party to check out the land offered to them by the government, which was mostly prairie. They did not like it and returned east with some disgruntled members heading off to Canada to live.

President Martin Van Buren joined the chorus of those who wanted the Ottawa removed. They left in three separate groups with the first departing by land September 27, 1832 with seventy-two people. On August 31, 1837, 174 more Ottawa left for Kansas—mostly the younger tribal members. Ironically, before they could head west, this group chose to travel eastward on a steamboat to the Ohio and Erie Canal port at the Cuyahoga River. Once boarded on canal boats, they traveled south to the Ohio River at Portsmouth. From this point they boarded another steamboat for St. Louis, eventually reaching a reserve in Kansas. Another 150 Ottawa remained in Ohio. Finally, on July 25, 1839, they too departed the state by steamboat, leaving just a handful of mostly elderly Ottawa who wanted to die in the Maumee River Valley.

Of all the Native Americans who came to Ohio country after a long absence in the 1600s, the Wyandot/Hurons remained the last tribe to stand their ground. By 1836, about 700 Wyandots were living on the Grand Reserve at Upper Sandusky and a second tract named Big Spring. The Wyandots were smart and adaptable people. They had taken the government's direction to assimilate into the American culture by becoming prosperous farmers and breeders of livestock. They grew crops and planted orchards. Their farms were well managed, and they wanted their children educated.

But the Wyandots had never hidden from a fight. They fought bravely against the British in the French and Indian War and with the British during the American Revolution—both times on the losing side. Those who had joined Tecumseh's confederacy lost the battle to the Americans at Fallen Timbers, but they did not lose hope for a better life. In the aftermath of that battle, however, the Wyandots acquiesced to the Americans and sought to obtain a more "civilized life." In the area there were settlers willing to assist them. The Quakers, for example, built saw and grist mills and showed the Wyandots how to run them. Methodists ministers, likewise, opened their doors to them.

In 1831, they were visited in Upper Sandusky by Col. James Gardiner. He had come to seek a deal for the Wyandots to leave Ohio. The chiefs sent a delegation of five men led by William Walker Jr. to see the land offered to them in the west. Walker's mother was a Wyandot and he had become a respected leader of the tribe. As they passed through Missouri, they were disturbed to find slave holders there who were also hostile to the tribes.

Walker returned to Ohio and told Gardiner there was no deal. Subsequently, (now Secretary of War) Lewis Cass appointed Ohio Gov. Robert Lucas as a commissioner to get the job done. Cass promised the Wyandots they could have any piece of territory in the Kansas territory equaling their 109,000 acres in Ohio plus possibly more. The Wyandots were still not satisfied. Lucas was told the Wyandots had taken a tribal vote and stubbornly refused to leave.

Bill Moose's Grave. Bill Moose's grave was created with thirty-nine granite boulders taken from the nearby Scioto River to form a teepee.

William Walker rose to the position of principal chief in 1836. He had been educated at a Methodist school in Worthington and spoke several languages. He was an excellent speaker and negotiator who always had the Wyandot's best interest at heart. Meanwhile, his ambitious tribesmen wanted to stay in Ohio and raise money toward improvements to their reserves. Walker went to the nation's capital to try to reach a deal to sell a piece of the Grand Reserve for cash paid directly to the chiefs. A squabble occurred when Congressman William Hunter of Sandusky stepped in to try and purchase the land. Walker rebelled saying the land, per treaty, had to be sold to the U.S. government and not to any one individual.

Some of the other chiefs such as Warpole wanted the purchase to go through. They wanted the revenue and they wanted to leave Ohio. Local government officials ultimately decided that individual Wyandots could sell their land to whomever they pleased.

On March 3, 1841, a Democratic Congress appropriated money to re-start the negotiations with John Johnston as the lead negotiator seeking the Wyandots removal. Johnston traveled to Upper Sandusky with the directive from President John Tyler to obtain all the land the Wyandots still owned. The offer was straightforward—the U.S. government would purchase the land in exchange for an equal amount of land across the Mississippi. They would also be given an annuity and other incentives to sweeten the pot.

The Wyandots were smart and they knew what they were facing. Ohio's population had gone from 42,159 in 1800 to 581,434 in 1820 to 937,903 in 1830. As the population of settlers swelled, the population of the Native Americans dwindled to almost nil. The tribe's natural instincts kicked in and they decided to return to a life of freedom that they were promised across the Mississippi.

The negotiations commenced. On March 17, 1842, the Wyandots voted to leave Ohio for Kansas and set about to organize their move. Part of the Wyandots' change of heart occurred after the brutal murder of Chief Summerundewat, his brother-in-law, and his wife in the hands of outlaws the previous year. On July 12, 1843, about 670 Wyandots plus some other tribal members from Michigan and Canada rolled out of Ohio with about 140 wagons and dozens of horses. All along the trail, people lined up to bid a solemn farewell. Eventually, Walker would become the provisional governor of the Kansas territory in 1853. He died there in 1874.

A handful of Wyandots stubbornly remained in the territory between Upper Sandusky and Columbus along the Scioto River. This river had served as their major

Close-up of the image on Bill Moose's grave. He is considered the last full-blooded Wyandot Indian to be born in Ohio (Wyandot County) and live there until his death.

highway taking them to tribal festivals, hunting trips, council gatherings, and to war.

Among those living along the river was the Wyandot family of Bill Moose Crowfoot. Bill was born in 1837 near Upper Sandusky. As a young man, Bill moved to the Dublin area, also known as Sell's Town, along the Warriors Trail 2. For many years he lived in a small hut in northern Columbus (the site of Wyandot Golf Course from 1923–1952). It was here that Bill taught Indian crafts and often wore native garments. For several years he worked for the Sell's Circus.

Bill Moose died at the age of 100 years and was buried in full ceremonial tradition in 1937. His tombstones consist of thirty-nine granite boulders stacked nine feet high that were taken from the nearby riverbed. It is formed into a teepee. On the top boulder is an image of a Native American and a settler shaking hands.

Bill is considered to be the last full-blooded Wyandot from the last of the great tribes that once prospered and built the groundwork for Ohio. Throughout the Buckeye state today, there are colleges, cities, townships, lakes, highways, bridges, parks, monuments, hospitals, school districts, businesses, and people (William Tecumseh Sherman) named after Native Americans who once lived within the state of Ohio's borders.

Bill Moose Crowfoot's tribal family had lived along the river for over 200 years. With his death, his home state lost an important part of its history. His grave faces the Scioto River.

Ohio's tribes may be gone but they will not be forgotten. These simple words are carved in stone below a petroglyph of Bill Moose's image, *"Last of the Wyandots. Born in 1837 and whose death in 1937 marks the passing by the Indians from the territory."*

> ### ➤ Additional Information
>
> Bill Moose's grave is located on State Rt. 33 on the east side of Riverside Drive near Lane Road four miles south of Dublin on what is known as Wyandot Hill.
>
> In 1924, Congress passed the Snyder Act granting citizenship to all Native Americans born in the U.S. who had not otherwise sought it. Up until the 1960s some states barred Native Americans from voting. It was not until the Voting Rights Act of 1965 that they all received full voting rights.
>
> The Indian Reorganization Act of 1934, or the Wheeler-Howard Act, has been called the "Indian New Deal." This act was designed to restore to Native Americans the management of their assets (land and mineral rights) and included provisions intended to assist with the economic aspects for those living on Indian reservations.
>
> Since 2020, all three Shawnee tribes—known as the Loyal Shawnee, Eastern Shawnee, and the Absentee Shawnee—have headquarters in the northeastern Oklahoma area. The headquarters for the Seneca-Cayuga tribe is also in northeastern Oklahoma, as is the headquarters for Wyandotte Nation. The Miami tribe's population is concentrated in northeastern Oklahoma, eastern Kansas, and northern Indiana. The Delaware have headquarters in both Oklahoma and Kansas.

14
Area Artifacts and Monuments

There is a wealth of Native American mounds, village sites, artifacts, and historical markers in the southwestern quadrant of Franklin County. Three of four mastodon remains found in the county were discovered in the Grove City area. As noted in Chapter 2, a mastodon skeleton was found behind St. John's Evangelical Lutheran Church in a tile pit in 1899. The Ohio Conservation Bulletin (now part of the Ohio Department of Natural Resources—Division of Wildlife) of September, 1963 states that partial remains of another mastodon was found at that same spot in 1920. A third was discovered on the S. Landes farm on (now) Hibbs Road near the Scioto River one mile west of Shadeville. The date on that find is unknown.

The Adena culture appear to have loved the Scioto and Darby Creek waterways. The Big and Little Darby Creeks feed into the Scioto at Circleville and head south to the Ohio River. It was a natural highway for these and the people to come later.

After Ohio became a state in 1803, Franklin County was divided into four townships with the entire southwest quadrant titled Franklin Township. In 1807, Pleasant Township was formed out of Franklin Township and was five times larger than it is today. In 1815, Jackson Township was formed from parts of Franklin and Pleasant townships. In 1819, Prairie Township was organized from parts of Brown and Franklin townships.

Studies have shown that Native American mounds and villages were in all four townships that incorporate Southwest Franklin County—Franklin, Jackson, Pleasant and Prairie townships, plus Brown Township north of Prairie.

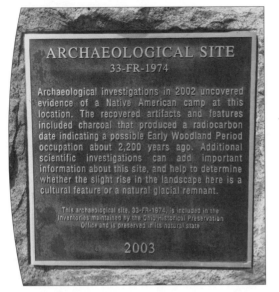

ARCHAEOLOGICAL SITE
33-FR-1974

Archaeological investigations in 2002 uncovered evidence of a Native American camp at this location. The recovered artifacts and features included charcoal that produced a radiocarbon date indicating a possible Early Woodland Period occupation about 2,200 years ago. Additional scientific investigations can add important information about this site, and help to determine whether the slight rise in the landscape here is a cultural feature or a natural glacial remnant.

This archaeological site, 33-FR-1974, is included in the Inventories maintained by the Ohio Historical Preservation Office and is preserved in its natural state

2003

This archaeological site memorial on Autumn Wind Drive in Grove City marks the place where Early Woodland Indians had a campsite 2,200 years ago. It was discovered during housing construction in 2002.

Mounds, monuments, markers, and artifacts found here include the following sites:

Ernie and Dorothy Good's collection of lanceolates (see Chapter 2): discovered in the 1950s near Stringtown Road at State Rt. 104. This historic find includes 250 whole and fragmentary lanceolates and stemmed lanceolate points. The discovery was so important that a point type, called the Stringtown Stemmed Lanceolate, was named for this location. Three distinct types were found there: 1) the classic stemmed lanceolates found on other Plano sites; 2) the Stringtown II variety which is less broad-bladed with a narrow stem and pronounced shoulders, and 3) the Stringtown III type which is characterized by a long and narrow stem. (Note: both types II and III may not be identified as Plano.) Nine pieces of the collection made of Flint Ridge flint are not commonly found in Plano sites. Most of the projectile points were made of Delaware chert.

Evidence of occupation during the Archaic period is seen in the collection of hammerstones and pitted milling stones. Rare atlati weights made of gneiss were also found.

Also found at the Stringtown Road site were Early Woodland artifacts including a tubular Adena pipe made of fine-grained sandstone. This piece is exceedingly rare because it is engraved. Also found were pieces of five gorgets which may

Grooved axes. Two ¾ inch grooved axes from the Archaic period were found on the Haughn farm on Haughn Road by Michael Haughn. Other items found include a hatchet and arrowheads.

be either Early or Middle Woodland and four plummets—two of which are hematite that are possibly Late Archaic or Early Woodland. A Hopewell platform pipe from the Middle Woodland period is also among the collection.

Archaeologists have concluded that the Stringtown location was a favorite prehistoric Native American campsite from the Paleo-Indian until Middle Woodland times. Some have even concluded that it marks the beginning of a transition from the Late Plano to Early Archaic period.

Milligan Mound: discovered just south of White Road and Hoover Road on the site of (now) Grove City High School east of the Athletic Center. The diameter is seventy-two feet E/W and forty-nine feet N/S. It stood 3.65 feet high. A two-inch long Adena stemmed point, a 3¾-inch grooved axe and a 1¾ inch triangular point were

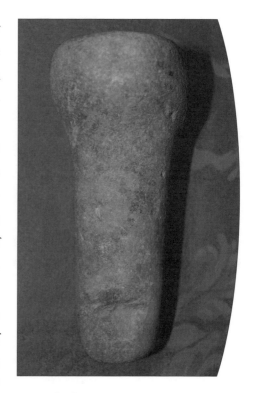

Bell pestle. This bell pestle from the Archaic period was found on the farm of settler Robert Worthington by Clark Worthington in Pleasant Twp.

removed from the mound site there. A small Ziegenspeck family cemetery from the 19th century was found on the same location. The Ziegenspecks were an early Grove City family who immigrated from Germany.

James Corry Mound: once located on the James Corry farm north of White Road between the Scioto River and St. Rt. 104. An 1883 map of Jackson Township shows the farm once was home to an Indian village. The map, published by G.J. Brand & Co., shows two other villages that were once slightly north of there. To the south of the property are six different mounds that head down to the Pickaway County line. In addition, the map shows five other Native American villages between Holton Road and the Pickaway County line.

A 1914 map by William C. Mills published by Fred J. Heer, shows twenty-one mounds in Jackson Township, including one on the west side of Harrisburg Pike between Rensch and Beatty Roads, one west of Demorest Road in the (now) Westgrove subdivision, and one east of Broadway along Marsh Run Creek. The same

Sea shell. This shell, probably used as trade by the Hopewell people, was found on the farm of Clark Worthington in Pleasant Corners.

set of maps show seven mounds to the north in adjoining Franklin Township, ten to the west in Pleasant Township, and twenty-five directly to the east in Hamilton Township.

Waller Mound: located on Clayton Ct. off Shawnee St. in the Indian Trails subdivision.

Unmarked Mound: located in northern Jackson Township off Marlane Dr. near I-270. This mound is located on private property and is not accessible.

Autumn Winds Drive Archaeological Site: a monument was erected at this location in 2003 stating a Native American camp was uncovered there in 2002 and is possibly from the Early Woodland Period of about 2,200 years ago. The location is about 1.5 miles west of the Scioto River.

Grant-Sawyer Homestead on Haughn Road: a pestle for grinding corn was found on the grounds by a member of the Grant family and passed down through generations. This home was built in the 1830s where the Grant family once farmed on the east side of Crushed Stone Pike (now Haughn Road). Hugh Grant Sr., a native of Pittsburgh, first explored the Scioto River in 1797 and seven years later purchased 450 acres of land that is now the center of Grove City. The original Grant home, a 1920s carriage house, and a 1920s barn have been restored by the city of Grove City and are open for tours by appointment.

Stringtown Road: arrowheads and other artifacts were found by the children of Stewart and Mae Gibboney on their Stringtown Road farmland during the 1930s–1950s.

State Route 665 near Scioto River (Hibbs Road): pieces of pottery, blue flint, and arrowheads were found by Boy Scout Troop 136.

Hammerstone. This prehistoric hammerstone was found on the farm of Clark Worthington in Pleasant Corners in Pleasant Township. Hammerstones were used to cause percussion fractures on another rock.

Trouble on Scioto's Waters

Old Haughn Farm on Haughn Road: stone axes and arrowheads were found on Haughn farm by Michael Haughn (dates unknown).

Stringtown Road Walmart Supercenter: a Hopewell bladelet was found during the construction of a Walmart Supercenter store in the 2000s at 1693 Stringtown Road in the Parkway Centre Shopping Center.

Sites in Pleasant and Prairie Townships

Worthington Farm: owned by John and Linda Worthington at State Rt. 665 and Harrisburg Pike in Pleasant Corners: artifacts found there include a bell pestle used to grind corn, a ¾-inch grooved axe, a hammerstone, and an assortment of arrowheads. One of the small arrowheads was used to shoot birds. Several of the items may be from the Archaic period.

Carl Graul Farm near Darbydale: a Native American red slate winged bannerstone (also known as a butterfly bannerstone) used as a counterweight on an atlatl was found at this site. An atlatl is a spear-like weapon thrown with a handle used to kill game or to use in battle. It was found near Darby Creek by Carl's son Charles Graul and is now owned by Mark Shaw.

Flint. This flint, most likely from Flint Ridge in Licking County and was found by Clark Worthington in Pleasant Corners.

Cherry Creek subdivision: arrowhead was found along Cherry Creek on Cherryhaven Dr. north of Hall Road in Prairie Township by Sue Hamilton. Cherry Creek is part of the Scioto/Big Run watershed.

Bird shot. This bird shot arrowhead was found on the farm of Clark Worthington in Pleasant Corners.

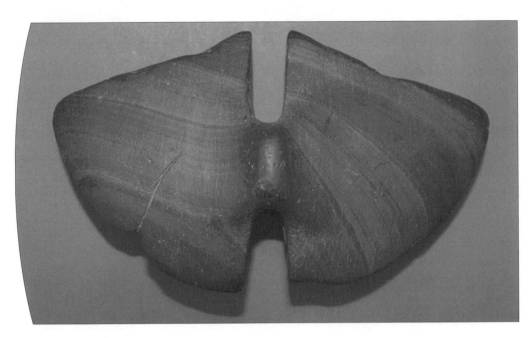

🔸 *Bannerstone. This rare red slate winged bannerstone, used as a counterweight for an atlatl by the Native Americans, was found along Darby Creek in Pleasant Township on the Carl Graul farm by his son Charles Graul. It is now owned by Mark Shaw.*

Sites in Brown Township

Old H.C. Adler farm: Brown Township near Darby Creek. An enclosure or fort was found there with two large circles of perhaps a half-acre of land. Its location was on a high bank of the creek. Numerous stone hatchets, arrow points, skinning knives and other artifacts were once found there, making it most likely a favorite camping ground for the Native Americans.

Old Henry Francis farm: Brown Township along Darby Creek. It once had a large mound and several smaller mounds which were believed to be burial mounds.

Prairie Oaks Metro Parks: Amity Road, Hilliard. Gravel burial mound along Mound Trail—culture unknown but possibly Adena.

Sites in Pickaway County

Farm of Pearl G. Johnson: a ¾-inch grooved axe and arrowheads were found in the 1950s along the east side of the Scioto River near South Bloomfield in Harrison Township. The items are now owned by his grandson Bob Johnson.

Trouble on Scioto's Waters

Lockborne area: several earthworks have been discovered near the Southerly Wastewater plant by LiDAR sensing technology east of the Scioto River.

Circleville area: previously unknown Hopewell earthworks were detected in the 2010s by LiDAR technology.

The following mounds and markers are found both in and near the 7,000-acre Battelle Darby Creek Metro Park in Pleasant and Prairie townships:

Parks Mound: on the west side of Big Darby Creek, west of Harrisburg-Georgesville Road and north of Gay Road.

The McMurray Mound Group: was

 Arrowheads. The arrowhead shown on the right is called a dovetail and is from the Archaic period. It was found in the 1950s on the farm of Pearl G. Johnson on the east side of the Scioto River in northern Pickaway County by his son.

found 400 yards east of Big Darby Creek within the confines of Battelle Darby Creek Metro Park. There were three mounds constructed in a straight line on a wooded ridge. All three were approximately 2.5 feet high. They are believed to be Adena.

The Montoney Mounds: was located on the east side of Big Darby Creek just east of old Harrisburg-Georgesville Road north of Haenzel Road.

The Sidner Mounds: were located on the second terrace along the west bank of Little Darby Creek slightly north of Geirich Road. Both Adena mounds were excavated by the Ohio Historical Society in 1962–63.

Voss Mound: located along the Ancient Trail. Fort Ancient Culture.

15
Walk the Walk

For those interested in areas where they can view the Scioto River, the Big Darby Creek, and Alum Creek in central Ohio, here is a list of public parks:

Antrim Park: 5800 Olentangy River Road, Columbus, Ohio, 43085. This 120-acre park is surrounded by a quarried lake and the Olentangy Greenway Trail. The lake is stocked with rainbow trout by the Ohio Department of Natural Resources.

Battelle-Darby Creek Metro Park: 1775 Darby Creek Dr., Galloway, Ohio, 43119. This park is 7,000 acres and stretches along thirteen miles of the Big and Little Darby Creeks where you can canoe or kayak. There are over 1,600 acres of restored wetlands and prairies. There are 800 acres open for hunting small game and water-fowl. There is a nine-acre natural play area that features a ravine, creek, and trees for kids and caregivers. You can view bison as the Native Americans once saw them from the Battelle-Darby Creek Metro Park Nature Center. Along Ancient Trail you can see a Fort Ancient Indian Mound named the Voss Mound.

Dublin Waterfall Tour: Visit Indian Run Falls, 700 Sharon Falls Dr., Dublin Ohio, 43017 and Hayden Falls, 4326 Hayden Run Road, Dublin, Ohio, 43017.

Glick Park: 1 Glick Road, Dublin, Ohio, 43065. This park has a great overlook of O'Shaughnessy Dam on the Scioto River.

Highbanks Metro Park: 9466 Columbus Pike, Lewis Center, Ohio, 43035. This park has 1,200 acres. It is named for a massive 100-foot high shale bluff towering over the Olentangy State Scenic River. There are deep ravines in the eastern part of the park.

James Thomas Park: 2933 Riverside Dr., Columbus, Ohio, 43221. Great view of the Scioto River.

Prairie Oaks Metro Park: 3225 NE Plain City-Georgesville Road, West Jefferson, Ohio, 43162. This park has 2,203 acres with 500 acres of flowering prairies, grasslands, and spectacular scenery of the Big Darby Creek. The Big Darby is a State and National Scenic River.

Schiermeier Olentangy River Wetland Research: 352 W. Dodridge St., Columbus, Ohio, 43202. This fifty-two-acre urban research site is next to the Olentangy River with two experimental wetland basins on the northern edge of The Ohio State University campus. Grounds are open to the public daily. The experimental wetlands can be viewed from the Sandfur Observation Pavilion.

Scioto Audubon Metro Park: 400 W. Whittier St., Columbus, Ohio, 43215. This 120-acre park off the banks of the Scioto River is a recreational and educational destination just south of downtown Columbus. The area was once a brownfield site now turned into a green oasis for birds and wildlife.

Scioto Grove Metro Park: 5172 Jackson Pike, Grove City, Ohio, 43123. This 620-acre park along the Scioto River has mature forests overlooking the scenic Scioto River. There are seven miles of trails plus canoeing, kayaking, and fishing. The Mingo Trail runs along the Scioto River.

Scioto Mile Promenade: 233 Civic Center Dr., Columbus, Ohio, 43215. This promenade is along the east bank of the Scioto River connecting Battelle Riverfront Park and Bicentennial Park along Civic Center Drive. There is a great scenic view of the riverfront available at Coleman's Pointe.

Scioto Park: 7377 Riverside Dr., Powell, Ohio, 43065. See the Chief Leatherlips Monument.

Three Creeks Metro Park: 3860 Bixby Road, Groveport, Ohio, 43125. This 1,100-acre park lies at the site of the confluence of the Alum, Big Walnut and Blacklick Creeks.

Other historical sites of interest in Ohio:

Adena Mansion & Gardens: 847 Adena Road, Chillicothe, Ohio, 45601. (740) 772-1500. Home of Thomas Worthington, the sixth governor of Ohio.

John Bryan State Park: 3790 St. Rt. 370, Yellow Springs, Ohio, 45387. (937) 767-1274. Limestone gorge cut by the Little Miami River.

Bucyrus Historical Society (Crawford County): The Scroggs House, P.O. Box 493, 202 S. Walnut St., Bucyrus, Ohio, 44820. (419) 562-6386. Call before you visit.

Delaware County Historical Society: 2690 Stratford Road, Delaware, Ohio, 43015. (740) 369-3831. Call before you visit.

Flint Ridge State Memorial & Museum: Heath, Ohio, 43056. (740) 763-4127. Displays of flint tools and points.

Fort Ancient: 6123 St. Rt. 350, Oregonia, Ohio, 45054. (513) 932-4421. North America's largest hilltop enclosure that was built 2,000 years ago. It is a National Historic Landmark.

Great Seal State Park: 4908 Marietta Road, Chillicothe, Ohio, 45601. (740) 887-4818. See the view that inspired Ohio's state seal.

Harrison House: 570 W. Broad St., Columbus, Ohio. See one of the first houses built in Franklinton where Gen. William Henry Harrison lived and used as his headquarters for the Northwest Army during the War of 1812. Tours not available.

Harrison-Symmes Museum, Cleves, Ohio, and the **William Henry Harrison Tomb**: 2 Cliff Road, North Bend, Ohio. North Bend was the home to both President William Henry Harrison and his grandson President Benjamin Harrison. Cleves is just north of North Bend, six miles from the Indiana border and fifteen miles west of Cincinnati.

Hopewell Cultural National Historical Park: 16062 St. Rt. 104, Chillicothe, Ohio, 45601. Earthen mounds and embankments built 2,000 years ago.

Logan Elm Memorial State Park: 4136-4498 St. Rt. 361, Circleville, Ohio, 43113. Location of the famous Logan Elm where Chief Logan delivered what is known as "Logan's Lament" to Gov. Dunmore. Historians have said the address was the most famous speech ever given by a Native American. The grounds include monuments to Shawnee Chieftainess Nonhelema (also known as Grenadier Squaw) and her brother Chief Cornstalk. The park runs along the Congo Creek.

Madison County Historical Society and Jonathan Alder Cabin: 260 E. High St., London, Ohio, 43140. (740) 852-2977. Call before you visit. The famous pioneer Jonathan Alder built his first cabin in 1806 along the Big Darby Creek in Madison (later Union) County. He is believed to be the first Anglo settler in Madison County. The cabin that sits on the grounds in London was moved there from Union County in 1935.

Miamisburg Indian Mound: 900 Mound Road, Miamisburg, Ohio, 45342. The second largest canonical mound east of the Mississippi. This ancient burial site is sixty-five-feet tall and sits above the Great Miami River.

Newark Earthworks: 456 Hebron Road, Heath, Ohio, 43056. (740) 344-0498. Largest set of geometric earthen enclosures in the world. It is the official prehistoric monument in the state. It is also a National Historic Landmark.

Pickaway County Historical Society: 162 W. Union St., Circleville, Ohio, 43113. (740) 474-1495. Call before you visit.

Pike County Museum: 110 S. Market St., Waverly, Ohio, 45690. (740) 947-5281. Call before you visit.

Piqua Historical Society: 9845 N. Hardin Road, Piqua, Ohio, 45356. Also visit Johnston Farm and Indian Agency in the summer. (937) 773-2522.

Portsmouth Earthworks Groups A and C: South Portsmouth, Ohio, and Greenup County, Kentucky. Not available to the public.

Portsmouth Horseshoe Mound Park: 1523 Grandview Ave., Portsmouth, Ohio, 45662. Unusual horseshoe shaped prehistoric mound built by Hopewell.

Ross County Historical Society: 45 W. 5th St., Chillicothe, Ohio, 45601. Call before you visit.

Scioto Trail State Park: 144 Lake Road, Chillicothe, Ohio, 45601. This 9,000-acre park has breath-taking views of the Scioto River Valley.

SunWatch Indian Village/Archaeological Park: 2301 W. River Road, Dayton, Ohio, 45417. (937) 268-8199. This park combines experimental archaeological research, including the reconstruction of Fort Ancient structures in their 13th century location. The park is on the National Register of Historic Places and is a National Historic Landmark. Open April–November.

Wyandot County Museum: 130 S. 7th St., P.O. Box 372, Upper Sandusky, Ohio. (419) 294-3857. By appointment only.

References

Alder, Henry Clay, *A History of Jonathan Alder and His Captivity & Life with The Indians*, Edited by Larry L. Nelson, Akron: University of Akron Press, 2002.

Anson, Bert, *The Miami Indians*, Norman: University of Oklahoma Press, 1970.

Butts, Edward, *Simon Girty—Wilderness Warrior*, Toronto: Dundurn, 2011.

Calloway, Colin G., *The Indian World of George Washington*, New York: Oxford University Press, 2019.

Converse, Robert & Good, Earnest, *The Stringtown Site & Stringtown Points*, Columbus: Archaeologist magazine, 1974.

Curry, W.L., *History of Jerome Township, Union County, Ohio*, Columbus: Heritage Books, 1913.

Durant, Pliny, *The History of Union County, Ohio*, Vol. I & II, Chicago: Beers, W.H. & Co., 1883.

Eckert, Allan W., *Blue Jacket—War Chief of the Shawnee*, Ashland, KY: Jesse Stuart Foundation, 2004.

Eckert, Allan W., *The Frontiersmen*, Boston, Little, Brown & Co., 1967.

Fitzpatrick, Stephen A., Ulysses Morris, *History of Columbus Celebration—Franklinton Centennial*, Columbus: New Franklin Printing, 1897.

Harvey, Henry, *History of Shawnee Indians, From the Year 1681 to 1854*, Cincinnati: E. Morgan & Sons, 1855.

Hale, James, Southwest Franklin County Historical Society website, Grove City: Mark Schmidbauer, Ed., 2019.

Howard, James H., *Shawnee! The Ceremonialism of a Native American Tribe and its Cultural Background*, Athens: Ohio University Press, 1981.

Howison, William, map of Early Ohio: Grove City, 1988.

Howison, William, *Reflections*, Grove City: Southwest Franklin County Historical Society, 1982.

Hurt, R. Douglas, *The Ohio Frontier: Crucible of the Old Northwest 1720-1830*, Bloomington: Indiana Press, 1996.

Hyde, George E., *Indians of the Woodlands: From Prehistoric Times to 1725*, Norman: University of Oklahoma Press, 1962.

Killikelly, Sarah H., The History of Pittsburgh—Its Rise and Progress, Pittsburgh: B.C. & Gordon Montgomery Co., 1906.

Lee, Alfred Emory, *History of the City of Columbus, Capital of Ohio—Vol. I*, New York: Munnrell & Co., 1892.

McGill, William A., *Ohio Indian Trails*, Kent: Kent State University Press, 2015.

Micklos, John Jr., *Tecumseh—Get to Know the Shawnee Chief Who Fought to Protect Native Lands*, North Mankato, MN: Capstone Press, 2019.

Milner, George, *The Moundbuilders: Ancient Peoples of Eastern North American*, New York: Thames & Hudson, 2004.

Mills, William C., *Archeological Atlas of Ohio*, Columbus: Ohio State Archaeological & Historical Society, 1914.

Murphree, Daniel, ed., *Native America: A State-by-State Historical Encyclopedia—Vol. II: Maine to Ohio.* Santa Barbara: Greenwood, 2012.

O'Donnell III, James H., *Ohio's First Peoples*, Athens: Ohio University Press, 2004.

Ohio State Archaeological & Historical Publications—Vol. I-X, Columbus: 1900, 1901.

Plain City, Ohio Historical Society website timeline—2014.

River, Charles, Editors, *Native American Tribes: The History & Culture of the Shawnee*, Lexington, KY: Charles Rivers Publishing, 2013.

Rowe-Schoolcraft, Henry, *Legends of the American Indians*, New York: Crescent Books, 1980.

Shailer, Janet and Laura Lanese,—*Images of America: Grove City*, Charleston, S.C.: Arcadia Publishing, 2008.

Skaggs, David Curtin and Larry Nelson, Editors, *The Sixty Years' War for the Great Lakes 1754-1814*, East Lansing: Michigan State Press, 2001.

Sugden, John, *Blue Jacket: Warrior of the Shawnee*, Lincoln: University of Nebraska Press, 2000.

Sutton, Kim, *Ottawas forced out of Paulding County*, Van Wert Independent, 1/27/20.

Swauger, James L., *Petroglyphs of Ohio*, Athens: Ohio University Press, 1984.

Swisher, James K., *Warfare History*, (Internet) 2018.

Tregillis, Helen Cox, *The Native Tribes of Old Ohio*, Westminster, MD: Heritage Books, 1993.

Vogel, John J., Ph.D., *Indians of Ohio's Wyandot County*, New York: Vantage Press, 1975.

Warfare History, Lord Dunmore's War: The Battle of Point Pleasant, Internet, Oct. 2018.

Woodward, Susan L. and Jerry N. McDonald, *Indian Mounds of the Middle Ohio Valley*, Granville: McDonald & Woodward Publishing, 2001.

Zimmerman, Dwight, *Tecumseh: Shooting Star of the Shawnee*, New York: Sterling, 2010.

About the Author

Janet Shailer was born and raised in Grove City, Ohio—an agricultural community set between the Scioto River and Big Darby Creek. She received a Bachelor of Arts degree with a major in Radio/TV/Film and a minor in journalism from Bowling Green State University in 1971. In her early career, Shailer worked as a broadcast engineer for two NBC-affiliated TV stations and Warner Qube's cable TV network. Later she worked as a videographer/writer/producer of public affairs programming for Columbus Community Cable Access. Her writing credits include working as a contributing editor for Television Broadcast magazine and writing for other national and regional magazines. She worked as editor of the *Southwest Messenger* newspaper for nine years and another five as a reporter/photographer.

Shailer is the author of two local history books for Arcadia Publishing—*Images of America: Grove City*, and *Images of Modern America: Grove City*, as well as one novel, *The Austerlitz Bugle-Telegraph: A King, A Goddess and a Chronicle of Deception* for Orange Frazer Press. In addition, she has self-published three children's books.

Her career awards include a Philo T. Farnsworth Award for cable TV programming, a national IFPA award for column writing, and the Humane Award for Distinguished Service from the Capital Area Humane Society for documentary writing.

Shailer serves as a member of the Board of Trustees for Southwest Public Libraries in southwest Franklin County, and is a member of the Ohio History Connection.

She and her husband John (Jack) live in Grove City. They have two adult children and three grandsons.